True Confessions of a Film Critic

Sept - 2013,

To KEITH

CBC

CHEERS !

Sept, 2013

TRUE

CONFESSIONS

of a Film Critic

Robert Fontaine

GSPH

GENERAL STORE PUBLISHING HOUSE INC.
499 O'Brien Road, Renfrew, Ontario, Canada K7V 3Z3
Telephone 1.613.432.7697 or 1.800.465.6072

www.gsph.com

ISBN 978-1-77123-034-6

Cataloguing data available at Library and Archives Canada

Pour Sylvie et David

The Films

Acknowledgements

I wish to thank the following people for helping in various ways to make this book a reality: all of the good folks at General Store Publishing House—publisher Tim Gordon, editor Chrissy Shannon, publicist Alison Roesler, and art director Magdalene Carson—for believing in the project and applying their considerable talents to bringing it to fruition; CBC Radio One host Alan Neal and *All in a Day* producer Caitlin Crockard for their sharpness, creativity, and ever-positive vibes; my dear friends Kathy and Kevin, Andrea and Eric (and the boys), Bianca et Marc (*vous êtes cool!*); Michael, Marissa, Jennifer, and Ron; my good buddy Luc who was always encouraging me to "write another one!"; Jacques Émond (film buff *sans pareil*); James, David, and John; *Ginette et Serge pour votre positivisme*; my mother and father for once upon a time taking me to drive-ins and letting me stay up all night; *Sylvie et David qui éclairent mes nuits et égayent ma vie*; to all of the talented people I have worked with at CBC Radio, and to all of the faithful, jovial, warm, and brilliant CBC listeners who have so graciously lent an ear over the years. This book is for all of you. *Merci mille fois.*

Introduction

I am attending a show in a local art gallery. The owner, who is in full schmoozing mode, leads me by the arm to a well-dressed forty-something lady and introduces me as "Robert Fontaine, the movie reviewer for CBC Radio." She looks at me, smiles pleasantly, and says, "Hello. I'm sorry. Are you on Radio Two? I always listen to Radio Two; I just love it. So, what's your favourite movie?"

My brain feels like it just hit a very large speed bump. Not again. I don't have a favourite movie. I have about a hundred favourite movies. There's no such thing as a favourite movie.

I immediately feel guilty. I am being a bore. She just wants to chat. I have to say something . . .

I smile back.

"No, I'm on Radio One. More talk, less Beethoven." I go on. "Well, you know a movie that I really love and that I've seen many, many times is *The Day the Earth Stood Still*—the 1951 science-fiction film with Michael Rennie and Patricia Neal, directed by Robert Wise. Have you seen that one?"

"1951? Really? Wasn't that with Keanu Reeves? He has an interesting face. Don't you like Beethoven?"

"No, Beethoven is lovely. Uh, the Keanu Reeves version was a remake. Actually, it wasn't even a remake—it was a TRAVESTY. I'd like to see everyone involved reduced to ashes by Gort's heat ray. Or maybe public stoning; the writer and director could be lapidated with VHS copies of the original."

She stares at the glass of wine in my hand. I suspect that she thinks I am drunk or out of my mind.

I try to redeem myself. "Keanu was good in *Dracula*, the Coppola one?"

"I never saw that; I hate that horror stuff."

I try for a little humour (very little): "I know what you mean, all that blood. I never drink . . . wine."

She looks at my glass again and says, "Oh, I do. In fact, I wouldn't mind some right now, if you'll excuse me. Very nice chatting with you."

There are three lessons to be gleaned from this anecdote:

1. It's a good idea to temper your passion when you are having a normal conversation with someone you've just met;

2. You learn a lot more by listening to other opinions than you do by voicing your own; and

3. Never quote Bela Lugosi to a stranger in an art gallery.

A much better answer to her question would have been, "I have a lot of favourite movies. What are some of yours?" thereby allowing the lady to express herself. That is what people like to do.

— — —

Here are some questions that I ask myself when I am trying to get a handle on a particular film:

1. What story is the film trying to tell? Is it realistic or fantastic? Is it a fable, a parable, or a "true" story? Is it well told, that is, is the script literate and engaging? Does the narrative move along smartly toward the finish line, or is it prone to wandering slowly down side streets and lingering in alleys? How does the movie compare with other films that have similar themes, characters, or preoccupations? If it is a retelling of a familiar story—*Dracula*, for example—does it contribute any fresh angles or insights?

2. How does the film compare/resonate with the rest of the director's oeuvre? How does it fit in his or her body of work?

3. How does the film connect with the social environment that spawned it? Is it commenting overtly on social or political events, or perhaps commenting on contemporary issues in an oblique or covert way (e.g., commenting on a contemporary war by telling us a story that is set in the First World War, or commenting on racism by camouflaging itself as a science-fiction story about aliens)?

4. Is it a morality tale, a cautionary tale, or pure escapism? Is the film perhaps propaganda? Can you identify a subtext (i.e., what is the film *really* talking about)?

5. What means has the director used to tell the story and how successfully have they been employed? How do all of the building blocks of film—cinematography, lighting, editing, set design, musical score, casting, special effects—conspire to effectively tell the story?

6. Is the director trying to tell us a story in the traditional sense? Perhaps the film is more of a character study, or a visual poem, or a more abstract, non-narrative work.

7. Whatever its shape or form, did the film work for me? Why?

As mentioned in my previous book, I see film criticism as an art form. I see it as creative nonfiction. It is not rocket science and there are no absolutes, except perhaps for the handful of films that have achieved universal critical consensus, such as *La grande illusion, The Seventh Seal, Citizen Kane,* and *The Godfather.* And here is an important thing to remember: movies change over time because we change. A film that you saw as a child is not the same film when you view it at age forty. It is, but it isn't. And let's not forget that great movies contain moments of magic, and magic is usually better left unexplained . . . unless you are in a film class.

If you are indeed faced with the daunting task of writing an essay in the context of a film class, professors invariably want nuts-and-bolts explanations of why, for example, the shower scene in *Psycho* is so effective. If you simply declare that "it was just magic," you will certainly be pressed to elaborate. So, the more you know about how movies work, the better equipped you will be to make interesting and engaging comments about them. And don't be afraid of going against the grain (or against the opinion of your friends or even the professor) when commenting on a film. Despite what some of our leaders seem to believe, dissent is not only extremely healthy, it is often extremely interesting. In the end, it is the quality of the proposed argument that stokes the fire of a stimulating conversation.

I've been very fortunate to have the privilege of expressing my opinions about movies on CBC Radio One for almost twenty years now. And I've also been fortunate to meet many CBC listeners over the years. I couldn't generalize about the listeners of any other stations, but I can tell you that CBC listeners are the sharpest, nicest bunch of people you could ever hope to meet.

Really.

To all of you reading this who are Radio One listeners—Radio Two listeners are nice folks also—and, more specifically, to listeners of *All in a Day*, I say thank you, thank you, thank you, for listening to my musings, opinions, ramblings, digressions, criticisms, witticisms (and the occasional half-witticism) over the years. To those of you who are not listeners but who are nevertheless movie lovers, I hope that some of the enclosed musings, opinions, and ramblings will engage and entertain you. And maybe even encourage you to tune in sometime.

Au plaisir.

Robert Fontaine
January 2013
Gatineau, Québec

2012

(2009)

In 2012 the Internet was rife with dire predictions about an impending global cataclysm. Proof that doomsday was just around the corner was provided by the ancient Mayan calendar that, it was claimed, ended on December 21, 2012. Cyber-doomsayers also claimed that the 2012 winter solstice would coincide with the alignment of the earth and the centre of the Milky Way in Sagittarius (or something equally obscure). I really can't remember the details, but it did occur to me at the time that the ancient Mayans could not possibly have known of this alignment when they drew up their calendar, unless Elvis had alerted them when he visited the Yucatan Peninsula in his flying saucer on his way to his vacation retreat in the Bermuda Triangle with Bigfoot.

In reality, the earth is always lined up in this way on the winter solstice and nothing ever happens, but where's the fun in that? To make things more interesting, some people decided that if the Mayans only calculated up to the date of December 21, 2012, it must be a clear indication that the world would end on that date.

I have another theory about the Mayan calendar and why it ended in 2012.

Ready?

They got tired of counting. Somebody grabbed the chief Mayan astronomer by the lapels and said, "Enough already with the calendar! We have a calendar that is good for the next five thousand years. Could we do something else now?"

This was of course not the first time that Armageddon was predicted, and it certainly won't be the last. I don't mean to minimize the genuine fear that some people feel when one of these scenarios is presented online or in the mainstream media, but we really do need to get a collective grip when it comes to this kind of stuff. My dog's licence expires every year on December 31, but my dog doesn't blow up on New Year's Day. Interestingly, Canadians never really got on the 2012 end-of-the-world bandwagon. Not that Canadians are smarter than anybody else; it's just that we have known for many years when the world will end. Canadians know that the world will end the next time the Toronto Maple Leafs win the Stanley Cup.

— — —

How much of a mess could you make if you had $260 million at your disposal? It's a pretty safe bet that anyone could really make a mess with that much money, but I think that it takes true genius — scintillating genius — to make a mess equalling the magnitude that is on display in Roland Emmerich's *2012*.

Emmerich makes messy movies. He is a master. He is the master of the messy movie. He gave us *Independence Day*, *Godzilla*, and *10,000 B.C.* — messes all. But with *2012* he has outdone himself. This may not be his *Titanic*, but it is a monumental dud. I read in his biographical notes that, as a student, Emmerich pursued painting and sculpture. Unfortunately for moviegoers, they eluded him.

The plot of *2012* incorporates elements of every disaster movie ever made. You have seen those manuals that have titles like *PCs for Dummies*. This is *Disaster Movies for Dummies*. Earthquakes, tidal waves, cities burning, cities freezing, world famous monuments burning up and freezing, huge ships taking on water and sinking, the president going down with the ship, and Los Angeles falling into the sea (while burning and freezing). It's all here — twice.

Emmerich borrows and steals from everything: *Titanic*, *When Worlds Collide*, *Armageddon*, *Independence Day*, *The Day After Tomorrow*, *The Poseidon Adventure*, *Earthquake*, *Annie Hall* — well, maybe not — *Deep Impact*, *Avalanche*; you get the idea. As a director, you know that you are in deep, deep trouble if you are borrowing from a movie as lame as *Avalanche.* When it comes to disaster movies, *Avalanche* represents the apex, the absolute summit of lameness. This is the movie that allowed Rock Hudson to utter the immortal lines, "It's tough getting to the top; it's always uphill!" Ain't it the truth?

John Cusack is the star of *2012,* and he spends much of the movie — which feels endless at two and a half hours — looking totally bewildered. Cusack portrays Jackson Curtis, an unsuccessful science-fiction novelist who is separated from his wife, Kate. Their two kids are living with Mom, and son Noah seems to have bonded with Kate's new partner, Gordon. Gordon is a plastic surgeon, as well as being something of a jerk, so as soon as he was introduced I started wondering how long he was going to survive. In the post-apocalyptic world, plastic surgery will not be an essential service, and jerks are always expendable. Another significant character is a young scientist named Adrian who is the first to understand that the earth's core is melting. I have come to expect bad science in disaster films, but *2012* offers the audience a voyage to the bottom of the scientific barrel. The dialogue is a veritable festival of gobbledygook. The explanation for the imminent disaster goes something like this: the neutrinos at the core of the earth are becoming superheated because of massive solar flares that are microwaving the earth's core (!). And if that isn't bad enough, the tectonic plates are shifting, the magnetic poles are reversing, the Thames has frozen over (in July), and I vaguely recall that there's even mention of rampant Dutch elm disease and a lockout in the NHL.

I'm quite fuzzy on the specifics, but trust me, things are looking very bleak for humanity. Not to mention the audience, which is quickly being submerged under a tsunami of pseudo-scientific gibberish.

Danny Glover portrays the president as a kind of old fogey who gets teary-eyed every ten minutes when he mentions his late wife, Elizabeth. He reminded me of Redd Foxx from *Sanford and Son.* Every time Redd faked a heart attack he would look skyward and call out to his dead wife, "This is the big one! I'm comin' to join you, Elizabeth!" Woody Harrelson shows up as a nutty talk-show host who has uncovered a massive conspiracy that is hiding the truth of the impending end of the world from people.

The ambitious (but totally inept) script features multiple characters and intersecting plot lines. Imagine a demented Robert Altman film, but with tidal waves. And just like an Altman ensemble piece, the big climax has all of the characters meeting—not at Wimbledon—but in the Himalayas. Incredibly contrived plot twists abound; for instance, Cusack's character works as a chauffeur for a rich Russian Mafioso whose girlfriend had cosmetic surgery at the hands of . . . Cusack's ex-wife's partner, Gordon! In another amazing coincidence, the young scientist Adrian is one of the very few people who read and enjoyed Jackson's latest novel, and they just happen to cross paths in Yellowstone Park. At this point I was hoping that the script would manage to work Yogi Bear into the story, but it never happened. Too bad.

At the heart of the inane proceedings is, of course, a conspiracy. The government knows that the end is coming, but to avoid panic it has orchestrated a massive cover-up. Even our scientist-hero is in on it. It is, in fact, a global conspiracy. In an effort to save humanity—although they aren't being too picky about who gets saved—all the governments of the world have conspired to build massive ark-like ships in China, and preparations are underway to load the ships with whoever can afford to pay the one billion euro cost of a ticket. The future looks even grimmer than we thought. It seems that only the rich and well-connected will survive. I have seen the future and it is populated by descendants of Donald Trump, Conrad Black, Sarah Palin, Alex Rodriguez, Mitt Romney, and the Russian Mafia. There goes the gene pool.

You may now be wondering if the movie's $260 million budget didn't at least buy some spectacular special effects. The short answer is no. The scenes of Jackson (Cusack) and family escaping the destruction of Santa Monica look like a bad video game: the family car swerves impossibly around collapsing buildings and jumps over giant cracks like one of those animated Hot Wheels in *Cars*.

In a disaster movie—as opposed to a disastrous movie—the disaster is ultimately only the backdrop that informs and shapes the human drama that is being played out. It is the depth of its humanity that makes a disaster movie gripping and memorable. The British classic *A Night to Remember* displays the full spectrum of humanity in all its contradictions — courage, cowardice, stupidity, and intelligence — showing us real people. In James Cameron's *Titanic*, a gigantic ship is going down, and a bunch of one-dimensional characters are allowed to spout insipid dialogue on their way to the icy depths.

Same disaster, huge difference.

I saw *Titanic* once and I don't feel the need to ever watch it again. It is a brilliant achievement from a technical point of view, but it fails to convincingly convey the human tragedy of the event. I have watched *A Night to Remember* many times, and it never fails to move me.

I feel sad because a whole new generation of moviegoers is being misled by filmmakers like Roland Emmerich. Subjected to movies like *2012*, the audience is in danger of forgetting that the most important ingredient in a successful disaster movie is the quality of the script. If the director cannot make you care about his characters, he is wasting his time. Even worse, he is wasting yours. Think of all the wonderful things you could do with those two and a half hours.

28 Weeks Later

(2007)

28 Weeks Later is the follow-up to director Danny Boyle's commercially successful 2002 zombie movie, *28 Days Later*. The previous movie told the story of a horrific biological plague that had been unleashed on the UK by animal rights activists after they had broken into a laboratory experimenting on monkeys. The highly contagious virus turned whoever was infected into a raging zombie who lusted for blood and the flesh of the living. *28 Days Later* was stylish, creepy, and extremely gory. This time around, the sequel is directed by Juan Carlos Fresnadillo with Boyle acting as producer.

Although as a genre the zombie movie never really went away, the last ten years have seen a major surge. The pitch culminated for me in 2006 with the release of the Canadian feature *Fido*, a totally demented film that inhabits a twilight zone that not even Rod Serling could have imagined — somewhere between *Night of the Living Dead* and *Lassie Come Home*. Cowritten and directed with great flair by Andrew Currie, this wacky gem reimagines 1950s suburbia as a place where the American (or Canadian) dream includes a car in every garage, a chicken in every pot, and a zombie to do the housework, babysit the kids, mow the lawn, and take out the garbage. Zombies have been domesticated thanks to radio-controlled collars, and young Timmy's best friend isn't the family pooch but rather the family's faithful six-foot-tall zombie who Timmy has named, appropriately, Fido — portrayed with great restraint by Scottish actor Billy Connolly. The script, cowritten by Robert Chomiak and Dennis Heaton, is very funny, creatively blending tongue-in-cheek (teeth-in-neck?) comedy, gore, and social satire. *Fido* has to be seen to be believed.

— — —

As *28 Weeks Later* begins, the plague is still raging and is decimating England. We don't know if Scotland has also been decimated but we assume so, although people who can eat haggis without suffering any significant side effects may well be immune to biological weapons. A small group of survivors is living near London in a barricaded house, subsisting on canned goods and living in dread as they anticipate the worst.

Not unlike how Toronto Maple Leafs fans feel before the start of every season.

A couple living in this barricaded house, Don (Robert Carlyle) and Alice (Catherine McCormack), are at least comforted by the fact that their two kids, twelve-year-old Andy and sixteen-year-old Tammy, are safe in Spain; they were on a school trip when the outbreak occurred in England. Very suddenly the house is attacked by crazed zombies and Don barely escapes, unable to save his wife from a horrible fate. Don makes his way to a safe camp set up by the US military and is later moved into a safe zone in London. Twenty-eight weeks later, his two children return to London, and life slowly returns to a semblance of normalcy. One day the kids sneak out of the American-controlled zone to return to their house a few miles away to pick up some personal belongings. Once at the house, they are surprised—terrified would be more like it—to see their mother alive and not a zombie. As we learn, there is something in her blood (and most likely also in her children's blood) that makes her immune to the virus. When another outbreak occurs, the family and a few others find themselves fugitives, running not only from the zombie hordes but also from the American military. By this point the US Army has decided that they are going to kill everyone, infected or not, because they can't tell who is hostile and who is friendly.

Suspense—real suspense—is a very difficult thing to create in a film. I know that it is difficult because so few filmmakers seem to have any idea how to do it. In lieu of creating suspense, the director of *28 Weeks Later*, Juan Carlos Fresnadillo, adopts a technique perfected by Michael Bay in *Armageddon*: he constantly jiggles the camera. In the early scene in the barricaded house suspense is almost created—until the zombies attack and the camera starts jiggling and moving around crazily all over the place. Worse, every time the zombies attack, not only does the camera jiggle and behave like a drunk on skates, but the editing becomes so choppy and fast and jerky that I started to feel nauseated and had practically no idea of what was going on. If theatres wanted to make a fortune with this movie, they should sell Gravol at the snack bar.

About twenty years ago when I first started reviewing films for CBC Radio, I complained that a scene in Abel Ferrara's *The Bad Lieutenant* was exploitative because the director showed a hypodermic needle being slowly pushed into an arm in close-up. In *28 Weeks Later* there is also a huge close-up of a needle being plunged slowly into an arm, but I hardly noticed because the woman's eyes were gouged out immediately after the needle went in. *The Bad Lieutenant* now seems pretty tame. An absolute splatterfest, *28 Weeks Later* also serves up helicopter rotors being used for mass decapitation, more eye gouging, and projectile vomiting of blood. Yuck-o.

Well, a lot of people like horror movies, and I like them, too. But at the risk of sounding old fashioned or unhip, I think that the horror genre has sunk to a dismal level. Contemporary horror movies—a lot of them—are suffering from another type of plague: second- and third-rate directors who have no idea how to create suspense and real chills, but instead are absolutely convinced that they need to throw buckets of gore in our faces. I am very, very tired of this.

Hello out there . . . would-be directors of horror films . . . hello? Stop splattering me with gore. Please. I can't focus with all that gore in my eyes, and I'm getting a headache, and my local drycleaners can't get all the blood stains out. Okay?

— — —

One explanation for the resurgent popularity of zombie movies is that they offer the writer and director interesting opportunities for social commentary. Indeed, there is often a social subtext to zombie films—symbolism abounds—and horror movies in general can often be read as parables. Case in point: a wonderfully weird and funny scene in George Romero's *Dawn of the Dead* takes place when a group of survivors is holed up in a shopping centre where the zombies are clunking around and groaning, as only zombies can, while shopping music cheerily plays in the mall. It is Romero's sharply satirical jab at mindless consumerism, and is easily the sunny highlight of what is an otherwise extremely bleak (not to mention gory) film. The fact that zombies are cannibalistic can also be read allegorically. When crazed consumerism is pushed to the nth degree and we have consumed everything around us in a frenzy of greed, all that is left to consume is (literally) your neighbour.

As I was watching *28 Weeks Later*, I could not help thinking about the war in Iraq. In the movie we have an American-led NATO force trying to bring peace and stability to a country after a terrible cataclysm. Survivors have been rounded up in a so-called green zone in the heart of London, while the outside perimeter is in chaos. When things go wrong, the American military uses extreme force indiscriminately because they can't tell who the enemy is anymore. Substitute the word "terrorist" for the word "zombie" and it seems pretty obvious. Don't get me wrong, *28 Weeks Later* is still a crummy movie, but it does at least have an interesting subtext. Every day seems to bring us more television images of sickening brutality. I was watching a baseball game on Fox the other night and I saw a commercial for extreme fighting with two guys trying to kick each other in the face. Now, that's entertainment! Brutality is increasingly marketed as entertainment, and it doesn't seem totally implausible to wonder if on some level *28 Weeks Later* isn't commenting cynically on this fact while at the same time exploiting our collective bloodlust. *28 Weeks Later* is a crummy movie, but it is also a revealing symptom of a profound malaise—a lust for blood—that is just under the surface of our so-called civilization.

Across the Universe

(2007)

Let's make it clear right from the downbeat—this movie celebrates the *music* of the Beatles, not the Beatles themselves. The Beatles are nowhere to be seen. In fact, the Fabs are not even mentioned in this movie. This is a vision of the sixties in which Beatles music is omnipresent and omnipotent, but in this parallel universe Beatles music exists without the group.

An age-old question comes to mind: which came first, the chicken or the egg, man? The normal way to begin a musical-film project is to come up with a story. Someone writes a story and someone writes some songs that punctuate the major dramatic events. But here the director has done it backwards. Julie Taymor first selected 200 Beatles songs, and then whittled that number down to thirty-three songs that she felt "best told the story of a generation and a time: the sixties." She continues, "The lyrics tell the story; they are the libretto, they are the arias . . ."

Unfortunately, this creative approach works about as well as a '68 Buick I used to own: in fits and starts. The movie offers up some great scenes; there are often spectacular and even exhilarating visual moments. Previously, Julie Taymor directed a movie about the artist Frida Kahlo that also contained some stunning visuals. She has also directed *The Lion King* on Broadway. Taymor has a great visual imagination, but the plot of *Across the Universe* is so contrived, incoherent, and riddled with clichés that it often becomes what we used to call "a real bummer." All you need is love? Well, maybe, but you also need a solid script that isn't constructed in such a way that it serves the songs instead of the other way around.

Early on when one of the characters, a young Asian woman,

is introduced as Prudence I thought to myself, gee; I wonder if at some point she is going to be really depressed and all of the other characters are going to gather around her and sing, "Dear Prudence, won't you come out to play? Dear Prudence, greet the brand new day-hey-hey-heyyyy." Yup.

At one point this character literally comes in through the bathroom window so that one of the characters can deliver the line, "She came in through the bathroom window!" Now *that's* clever. It is very much to the director's credit that the cast refrains from launching into, well, a refrain at that point. I am positive that I would have left the theatre if they had.

Confession time: I don't like musicals much to begin with. That being said, *Across the Universe* is not nearly as mind-numbingly annoying as *Rent*. But it's also not nearly as good as *Jesus Christ Superstar*, although it does try to do for the sixties what *JCS* did for the New Testament (i.e., make something that seems antiquated relevant for kids now). Ultimately I think that's a noble task.

You will enjoy this movie much more if you were not around in the sixties. The clichés won't seem so enormous, and the entire feel-good, flower-power, up-with-people groovy vibe won't seem so contrived and artificial. And if you weren't alive in the sixties you won't even be bothered by Bono portraying a character named Dr. Robert—a kind of LSD guru à la Ken Kesey—and singing "I Am the Walrus." Well, at least Bono can sing, which is far better than Jim Carrey warbling through "I Am the Walrus" like he did on that very weird George Martin–produced album a few years ago, which I now suspect was actually a thinly camouflaged comedy album (Sir George's very dry idea of a joke). But even Jim Carrey's warbling is infinitely preferable to William Shatner warbling "Lucy in the Sky with Diamonds." There is warbling and then there is w-a-r-b-l-i-n-g. Never mind the (very real) dangers of mind-altering chemicals; one listen to Shatner's vocalizations could permanently damage your chromosomes.

The plot, such as it is, of *Across the Universe* concerns a young Liverpudlian named Jude. It is 1963 or so, and our hero Jude is working in the dockyard and everything is very dreary and British. So he gets a job on a ship sailing for America, "seeking

11

adventure" he tells his mum. But in reality he has decided to track down his father, an American soldier who returned to the States at the end of WWII, never to be heard from again. It turns out that his dad is a janitor at Princeton University, and Jude eventually meets up with him. Their relationship has nowhere to go, but Jude does make a great new friend: a soon-to-drop-out-of-college hell raiser named Max. Jude and Max decide to head off to Greenwich Village in New York to experience the bohemian lifestyle. By now I believed that it was 1966, but as far as chronology goes, this is a jumbled movie. There is a race riot at one point but it seemed early to me—the Martin Luther King assassination would not have happened yet. It's all a bit confusing, but it wouldn't be the sixties if it wasn't confusing, dig?

Our heroes Jude and Max are joined in the Big Apple by Max's sister Lucy, and Jude and Lucy fall in love. Other characters include the aforementioned Prudence, the landlady Sadie, a blues singer who is the obligatory Janis Joplin surrogate, and also a black guitar player named Jo-Jo who is obviously modelled on Jimi Hendrix. In no time, everyone is caught up in the anti-war movement, Max is drafted, everyone discovers psychedelics, the music gets louder, the war escalates, the students riot, the culture collectively has a bad trip but . . . everyone is reunited in a happy ending as Jude sings "All You Need Is Love" in an impromptu rooftop concert that parallels that rooftop concert that was given by that other band that I can't quite remember the name of.

Can you dig it?

By this point, dear reader, you may well have concluded that I hated watching *Across the Universe*, but I didn't. Let me qualify that. I hated some of it, but I thought that some of it was brilliant. The film is so incredibly inconsistent that it seems like it was conceived especially for DVD; I could see every place where I wanted to skip to the next scene. As good as some of the musical numbers are—and some of them are brilliant—they barely saved the movie. Although the cast generally sing well, these new versions of classic Beatles tunes are hit and miss. One of the best hits has

Joe Cocker singing "Come Together" dressed in turn as a homeless person, a hippie, and a pimp. Mr. Cocker has lost none of his power and inspired growl. Another scene that works is at the army recruiting station when a large poster of Uncle Sam comes to life and launches into "I Want You . . . I Want You for the US Army." This is an effective, surreal scene. A quiet version of "A Day in the Life" played on the soundtrack by Jeff Beck also works well. But overall, the film is little more than a series of loosely connected music videos. A warning to teenagers: if you go with your parents and Mom and Dad leave the theatre saying things like, "yeah man, that's exactly how I remember it, the sixties . . . yeah" then you have to suspect that Mom and Dad may be having a flashback. Don't worry. They'll get back to normal soon. Just let it be.

Adaptation

Postmodernism

(2002)

The subject today is self-referential art. *Adaptation* is a movie that never lets you forget that you are watching a movie. It's always drawing attention to its own devices. Which is pretty rude if you think about it.

But making a spectacle of yourself—in an artsy way—can be a lot of fun if it's done right, although it can also become a bit of a copout, if not a bore after a while. But what do I know; I like Westerns and sci-fi B movies.

If you believe that art should be invisible, or rather that the means by which art is created should be invisible—that art should be artless—or if you simply go to movies to lose yourself in the story, then this movie might give you acid reflux (which, by the way, used to be called heartburn before the pharmaceutical companies realized that giving fancy scientific names to very ordinary problems allowed them to charge a lot more for their products).

When I first saw this it was at an advance screening in a packed theatre, and there was a gentleman sitting behind me who kept mimicking all of the sounds that the actors were making on the screen. He seemed almost delirious, happily beeping and buzzing and humming through the whole movie. This doesn't have anything to do with the movie per se, but I thought I would tell you about it because I want you to share my experience. Now do you realize what I have to put up with sometimes?

— — —

First of all, let me say that I sympathize with the screenwriter, Charlie Kaufman. I often stare in panic at my blank computer screen and wonder, "how the heck am I going to write a review about this movie?" And I have often been tempted to make the review about the process of writing the review rather than making the review about the movie I'm supposed to be reviewing.

Right about now, there should be a voice-over, my voice, saying,

> I'm sweating now; thank God nobody can see me sweating . . . I don't have anything interesting to say. I don't even think that I really understand this movie. Maybe I could talk about baseball and pretend that I'm referring to the movie, and maybe I can fool everybody. God, I'm losing my hair and I have no idea what I'm talking about . . .

This is the kind of voice-over we get in *Adaptation*. The main character, who is based on the real-life screenwriter Charlie Kaufman, is struggling mightily to write a script. And some of his musings are very funny. Essentially, *Adaptation* functions on not one, not two, but three levels; hence all of the references to the number three peppered throughout the film.

This is the story of an insecure, dysfunctional writer — I identified immediately with this character — struggling desperately to write a screenplay adapting a novel called *The Orchid Thief*. Note: *The Orchid Thief* is a real novel, written by a real writer named Susan Orlean, portrayed here by Meryl Streep.

In flashbacks we are plunged into the novel itself, which tells the story of a man named John Laroche (Chris Cooper) who steals and clones rare orchids to sell them to collectors. So we have a story within a story, but everything is running on parallel lines. The various narrative strands are on a collision course as we watch the movie that Charlie is writing. Eventually, time and space coincide and things come to a head (or two) because Charlie (played by Nicholas Cage) has a twin brother named Donald (also played by Cage), and they are often interacting in the same scene together.

Do you feel the room spinning, spinning, ever so gently?

Charlie is the insecure, dysfunctional brother; Donald is the confident, brash, loudmouth who is also writing a screenplay—a cliché-ridden, violent, silly screenplay—that is bound to have all of the success that Charlie's screenplay will not.

At this point you may be thinking that this all sounds terribly convoluted. The great strength of this film is that it does not sink under the weight of its many self-referential, non-linear narrative devices. It never loses its compass. I don't want to give the ending away, but I will say that in the end, *Adaptation* dares to borrow many of the so-called Hollywood devices it condemns in order to wrap things up in a slam-bang finish. Some viewers will be dissatisfied with the ending, but I think that for mainstream audiences, the ending saves the movie by giving the audience a much-awaited payoff. It could also be argued that in the end, *Adaptation* becomes exactly the type of film it has spent the preceding ninety minutes condemning.

— — —

> *I made up my mind, but I made it up both ways.*
> —Casey Stengel

Casey, I agree. *Adaptation* is smart and full of interesting ideas, but not entirely successful. It smacks a bit of what the hero tends to do at night when he's lying awake: intellectual masturbation. On the surface it seems highly original, but this device of having the writer put himself into the story is nothing new, and could be seen as a kind of copout. And if the novel you are trying to adapt for the screen is too challenging, then why not try adapting a novel that you can get a handle on? That being said, maybe there's something else going on here.

Back to square one: what is this movie *really* about? It's about writer's block. And it could be seen as a kind of homage to the Coen brothers' *Barton Fink*; but it also owes a debt to David Lynch, and to Robert Altman's *The Player*, and probably even to *Singing in the Rain* when you get right down to it, as far as self-referencing goes. But if you look at David Lynch—the first thing that strikes you is his hair of course, but look beyond that to his *films*—he never tries to explain anything that happens, no matter how profoundly bizarre. He doesn't care if you don't get it, or indeed if there's anything to get, which is why I liked *Mulholland Drive* so much. *Adaptation*, on the other hand, explains itself to death. That is its raison d'être. It's a movie about the creative process; one man's very public dissection of his own intellectual inadequacies. It could have been called *Being Charlie Kaufman*.

But there's more. It's also about the search for passion. We are all busy bees, the movie tells us, looking for our orchids. And that's ultimately everyone's struggle: to find something (or someone) to be passionate about.

There are two kinds of characters in this movie. There are the ones who are truly alive, like John Laroche, who are in touch with nature and take life as it comes and are not afraid to get their hands dirty. And then there are all of the intellectuals, like the novelist Susan, who paint themselves into mental corners, and are so busy analyzing and being self-consciously intellectual that they talk themselves out of living before they've even done anything.

I don't want to put words into Kaufman's mouth, but isn't that one of the main problems of the information age we live in? We have replaced action with thought. We are living under the illusion that thinking about something is somehow a substitute for really doing something about it. But then, is making a film about writing a screenplay just another example of mental gymnastics?

Adaptation is entertaining, but it's a one-trick pony. Once you get the joke, where do you go? I was alternately annoyed and entertained, sometimes in the same scene. It's like that really clever kid in grade school who knew all the answers and who was fond of pointing out how clever he was. He got good grades but he didn't make many friends.[1]

I detect two ironies here: the conventions of Hollywood that Kaufman condemns are the same ones he resorts to when he doesn't know how to get out of the mental corner he's painted himself into, and the intellectuals who bear the brunt of Kaufman's satire will be the ones to champion this movie while dissecting it over brunch.

---

1   Not an autobiographical comment.

Angel

Postmodernism

(2007)

François Ozon's film *Angel* is based on the 1957 novel *The Real Life of Angel Deverell* by Elizabeth Taylor.

No, not that one. The other one.

I am referring to the British novelist and short-story writer who died in 1975. Taylor the writer is not as well known, but she is highly regarded in literary circles and considered by many to be underrated. It could never be said of Liz that she was underrated.

The film tells the story of Angel Deverell. Although physically attractive, she is a rather dislikeable young woman. She lives in humble surroundings with her mother in a dingy town in Edwardian England. Angel lives in her own fantasy world. She believes herself to be supremely talented, and one day decides to send a novel she has written to a publisher. She then waits, and waits, for a reply. One day she is lying in bed, playing sick and refusing to go to school, when to her surprise she receives a letter from a London publisher saying that her manuscript is suitable for the market. This is hardly a ringing endorsement, but it's enough to set Angel off like a fireworks display.

She loudly declares to her skeptical mother that she is going to be a famous romance novelist. She travels to London to meet the publisher who is surprised that the author of such a lurid romance novel is a pretty young woman. He says to her, "I was expecting an old lady living in a cottage perhaps, or a middle-aged, bald-headed man; we receive a lot of work under pseudonyms." When he asks her if she reads a lot, Angel answers, "no, I don't have time." When pressed for a favourite author she declares, "I like Shakespeare except when he's trying to be funny." When the publisher suggests a few minor changes—she has one of her characters opening a bottle of champagne with a corkscrew—Angel is shocked. "I won't change a word or comma," she declares flatly. Who does she think she is, Stephen King?

In the next scene, our poor Angel is crying at the train station when the publisher comes looking for her to apologize for having requested changes to her manuscript. Being a published author myself and not unaccustomed to compromise, I immediately became dizzy and almost fell out of my seat. A story that has a publisher apologizing in this manner is obviously taking place not in Edwardian England, but most likely in a galaxy far, far away.

Soon, Angel's melodramatic romance novels become best sellers. She has everything she wanted: fame, fortune, and she meets a young woman named Nora and her brother Esmé who both eventually fall in love with her. Angel marries Esmé and Nora becomes her adoring secretary. World War I breaks out and in true romance-novel style, Angel's world falls apart. This is a classic rags-to-riches-back-to-rags story with tragic characters, overflowing with raging emotions, and dare I say it, raging hormones.

In 2003 I reviewed François Ozon's *Swimming Pool*, which I enjoyed very much. *Swimming Pool*, which starred Charlotte Rampling as a romance novelist, was a first-rate, postmodern thriller. With *Angel*, Ozon is aiming for postmodern melodrama. In Ozon's universe, a character's subjective perception can easily blur or collide with objective reality. *Angel* is done in the style of an old movie, and far from attempting to camouflage its artificiality, it celebrates it. From the first scene the overblown, retro-romantic music assails us, sounding a bit like "Love Is a Many Splendored Thing." The music is by Philippe Rombi, who also composed the score for *Swimming Pool*. His score would not be out of place in William Wyler's 1939 adaptation of *Wuthering Heights*—the music is ubiquitous and attention grabbing, creating an effect of heightened artificiality to constantly remind the audience that the events unfolding onscreen are overblown, satirical, and campy. It is as if the characters in the film are living inside one of Angel's tempestuous romance novels. When a thunderstorm arrives (on cue) to drench the characters who are having a raging argument, it is a sight to behold: a brilliant counterpoint to the onscreen histrionics. Other postmodern elements include rear-screen projection work that is cheerfully phony.

So why does the director want the audience to be acutely aware that what they are watching is not only fake, but kitsch? Ozon obviously loves old movies. Like Todd Haynes, who directed the brilliant *Far from Heaven* (2002) as a postmodern homage to Douglas Sirk and three-hankie movies, Ozon has studied the masters of melodrama and takes it one step further by drawing attention to the artificiality. Now that technology has made it possible to make even the wildest things look real, artificiality becomes a stylistic choice. Ozon is challenging us by saying, "look; look how phony this all is! But I will still draw you into the story even as I underline what a put-on it is." His enthusiastic embrace of artificiality allows him to upset our expectations, to set fire to all of the clichés we associate with melodramas, or to wallow in them. For example, the main character is not the tragic heroine who we normally find in these movies: the person who is too good and true and noble for this world. Rather, Angel is a self-centred, manipulative woman-child. She is the antithesis of the romantic heroine, and her character is brilliantly portrayed by Romola Garai who received a standing ovation at the Berlin Film Festival after a screening of *Angel*. Sam Neill portrays the publisher who sees the financial potential in Angel's marshmallow prose, and who also falls in love with her. No matter what role he plays, Sam Neill has always looked to me as if he just woke up from a deep sleep and hasn't yet had his coffee. But he is letter-perfect as the rather stodgy and phlegmatic publisher. Charlotte Rampling plays his wife. It is a small role, but Rampling—who was also superb in *Swimming Pool*—makes the most of her screen time. The entire cast is excellent.

Angel works on many levels, but perhaps best as a very amusing rant about the power of financial success to overwhelm artistic merit and critical judgment. Of course in the real world, crummy, overblown, and overwritten novels almost never become best sellers. François Ozon is a witty and original filmmaker, and while *Angel* is not a perfect movie, it is a wickedly funny one.

The Adventures of Tintin: The Secret of the Unicorn

(2011)

I think that it is difficult—no, make that impossible—for a non-francophone to grasp the enormity of what we are dealing with here. Tintin is beloved in the French-speaking world. For francophones the world over, Tintin is as famous as Bugs Bunny, Superman, and Peter Pan, combined. Even though Tintin is a Belgian creation, he is still considered "one of us" by francophone kids from dozens of nations, including Canada. He is one of the very few cartoon heroes of the francophone world, and by far the most celebrated. Generations have grown up with him, sharing in his adventures. One of my earliest memories is of sitting on my grandfather's knee—I was perhaps five—while he read a Tintin storybook to me. I remember vividly that it was *Le lotus bleu*, and I can still see the balloons over the character's heads, filled with black squiggles that meant nothing to me.

Back in the sixties, every kid I knew was an avid reader of the Tintin graphic novels, which were so colourful and richly illustrated—filled with eccentric and memorable characters like Capitaine Haddock, Professeur Tournesol, and, of course, the faithful dog Milou. And for a middle-class kid growing up in boring suburbia, Tintin's adventures were like a magical door opening to amazing, exotic times and places: Shanghai in the 1930s, Egypt, the Middle East, and even the moon, as Tintin had been the first human to walk on the moon in a graphic novel published in 1954. Reading these wonderful comics as a child, I fantasized that my later life would resemble Tintin's; that I would also have exciting adventures in the company of wonderful friends and (perhaps) a smart and faithful little dog. When I turned seven, I did get a smart little dog that resembled Milou (a little white terrier named Trixie) and she was a faithful friend for many years—always by my side and barking excitedly when the family backyard was transformed into Egypt or the moon.

This is not the first time that Tintin's adventures have made it to the big screen. Two live-action films were made back in the sixties: *Tintin et les oranges bleues* (Tintin and the blue oranges) and *Tintin et le mystère de la toison d'or* (Tintin and the mystery of the golden fleece).

They were awful.

I remember going to see *Les oranges bleues* one Saturday afternoon in a theatre filled with kids. I was about ten years old and very excited, as were all of the kids in the theatre, that my hero was about to appear in a movie. The movie started (finally) and all of the kids held their breath as the title appeared onscreen: *Tintin et les oranges bleues.* I looked questioningly at my friend André. The blank look on his face told me that he had never heard of this adventure either. Things quickly went downhill from there.

As much as we all loved Tintin, and wanted desperately to enjoy this film, it didn't take us more than about ten minutes to realize that we had been saddled with a stinker. Rather than adapt one of the well-loved (and well-written) graphic novels, the producers had chosen to go with an original script that was as corny as it was unexciting. The characters weren't too bad, though: an unknown twenty-something non-actor named Jean-Pierre Talbot had been selected by Hergé himself (Tintin's creator) to portray the young, daring reporter, and he was the spitting image of our hero. But that was not enough to save the movie. It is a tribute to Tintin's fame that to this day, Jean-Pierre Talbot—who is now about seventy years old—still receives dozens of fan letters every week addressed to Tintin.

Tintin has also been portrayed numerous times in cartoons. I remember a series of wretched, poorly animated Tintin cartoons that became a staple of kids' television in French Canada back in the sixties. They were broadcasted on kids' shows after school, and as awful as they were, we all used to run home to tune in because it was incredibly exciting to see our hero come to life, even if it was only in a cheap and herky-jerky cartoon. When I first heard that a big-time Hollywood producer was going to make a Tintin movie with an estimated $130 million budget and state-of-the-art motion capture technology, I was both excited and filled with dread. The advance marketing on this film was enormous, and by the time of its release in 2011, Steven Spielberg's *The Adventures of Tintin: The Secret of the Unicorn* had been keeping fans around the world buzzing for at least two years.

Spielberg says he discovered Tintin while making the first *Indiana Jones* film. When I saw *Indiana Jones*, I immediately thought it was heavily influenced by Tintin. And why not? Hergé was also influenced by American films of the twenties and thirties, particularly action films and cliff-hanger serials, so both he and Spielberg are drawing from the same creative well.

The Adventures of Tintin: The Secret of the Unicorn is adapted from a two-part Tintin graphic novel. Volume one is called *The Secret of the Unicorn*, and volume two is *Red Rackham's Treasure*, first published in 1942 and 1944, respectively. The screenwriters, Steven Moffat, Edgar Wright, and Joe Cornish, have actually taken parts of a previous Tintin adventure, *The Crab with the Golden Claws*, and woven it into the narrative in order to give us the backstory of how Tintin first met the salty and alcoholic Captain Haddock who will become his inseparable companion through numerous adventures. *The Secret of the Unicorn* is a mystery story involving three ship models—models of the *Unicorn*, a flagship under the reign of Louis XIV that was captained by Haddock's ancestor the Chevalier de Haddoque. When Tintin buys one of the models at a flea market one day, he is confronted by several characters who are interested in purchasing it from him. Describing themselves as collectors, they are even ready to pay much more than Tintin's purchase price. Our young reporter is of course immediately suspicious and refuses to sell. When his flat is burglarized and the model stolen, the wheels of intrigue are set in motion, and soon one of the would-be purchasers is gunned down at Tintin's front door.

What is the secret of the *Unicorn*? Could this ship model lead to the fabulous treasure of the pirate Red Rackham who was killed centuries ago in mortal combat with Haddock's ancestor? And where is the treasure? At the bottom of the ocean in the wreck of the *Unicorn*, or perhaps closer at hand?

Hergé's original stories are terrific. It is not by accident that they have remained popular with generations of readers. They are superbly constructed and suspenseful. Unfortunately, the screenplay at hand is a good news, bad news proposition. As a lifelong Tintin fan, it drives me to distraction that so many liberties have been taken with the original story. I don't mind incorporating the backstory of Tintin's first encounter with Haddock into the narrative, but the script should have followed the chronological order of events—it would have made a lot more sense.

In the original graphic novel, Tintin buys the ship model at the flea market as a birthday present for his friend Haddock. We then discover all of the mystery and the links to Haddock's ancestor. But here, Tintin buys the model before he has even met Haddock; he buys it out of curiosity. This bothered me. I found it an illogical and frankly unnecessary change, and it is only one of many modifications to the original storyline that I found at best superfluous, at worst overly convoluted. Hergé's original stories are models of economy and narrative propulsion. Why fiddle with them?

The character of Sakharine, a minor figure in the original comic, becomes the major villain. And to inject a note of the supernatural into the story, Sakharine is presented as the reincarnation of the evil pirate Red Rackham—locked in a centuries-old war with Haddock.

I couldn't believe it. The supernatural plot twist brought me back in time to the terrible disappointment I experienced in that movie theatre long ago . . . it was happening again! All that was missing were the blue oranges zinging by my head in state-of-the-art 3D. For me, this major tinkering with the storyline was a bit like adapting Jane Austen by having Emma take a trip to Egypt to discover that she is the reincarnation of Cleopatra. Okay, Hergé is not Jane Austen, but why all this tinkering? How would Spielberg feel if *Jaws* was remade into a sci-fi film with E.T. as a stowaway on Quint's boat?

Spielberg has also turned Tintin into a kind of Indiana Jones action hero, with an overabundance of wild action and chase scenes. Some will say that these action scenes are absolute marvels of virtual imaging—and there is no doubt that the digital technology involved is impressive—but even too much Dom Pérignon will give you a headache. My head was spinning. The violence has also been cranked up several notches, and one scene where Haddock's crew is sent to their watery graves may prove too much for young children. Was all of this necessary to bring Tintin to life?

On the plus side (yes, I do have something positive to say about this) the movie is, for the most part, a visual delight. Right off the bat, the opening credits are terrific. I haven't seen opening credits this attractive since those old Pink Panther movies. In the opening scene, a cartoonist at an outdoor flea market is drawing a caricature of a character that we only see from the back. The cartoonist turns and we recognize Hergé. He holds up the drawing he has made—the cartoon Tintin we all know—and then the subject turns to face us and we recognize the new Tintin (the cartoon Jamie Bell). It is a lovely moment.

Andy Serkis—the master of motion capture—is excellent as Haddock. Simon Pegg and Nick Frost as the bumbling Thompson detectives is an inspired bit of casting, and they provide some amusing moments. But the star of the show is Snowy (Milou, for the francophones). This is a glorious portrayal of Tintin's lively, feisty, loyal, and intelligent canine companion. With the incredible advancements in computer-generated imagery (see the amazing tiger in 2012's *Life of Pi*), the Academy of Motion Picture Arts and Sciences should think about adding a special effects category, Best Achievement in CGI Character or Animal. Snowy would have won hands down in 2011.

My son was twenty when we saw this together, and although he also grew up with Tintin, he had not had the benefit (or perhaps the disadvantage) of decades of exposure to the graphic novels. Consequently, he did not have nearly as many bones to pick with Spielberg as his old dad did. Purists will find much to fault with Spielberg's plot excursions, but many will also be thrilled that it was done so well.

Appaloosa

Night of the Living Western

(2008)

Some things die hard. You think they are dead and buried, but they pull a zombie on you—they get back up out of the grave and chase you down the road. There are lots of examples: Reaganomics, that "trickle-down" voodoo stuff that never seems to stay buried; the 2004 Boston Red Sox who returned from the grave in game four of the American League Championship Series to murder the Yankees; and Bruce Willis—he dies hard.

The Western has been pronounced dead many times over the course of the last fifty years. In the 1960s, after many leading critics and film aficionados had loudly (and somewhat pompously) described at great length how the American Western was as relevant as the steam engine, *Butch Cassidy and the Sundance Kid* was a box-office smash and took home four Oscars in 1970. Hey, hey, my, my; Western movies will never die.

Sorry, Neil.

The Western resurfaced spectacularly in 1990 when Kevin Costner saddled up for *Dances with Wolves*. In case you've forgotten, Costner's epic won seven Academy Awards, including Best Picture. And Clint Eastwood blasted through the door in 1992 with *Unforgiven*, which again confirmed the rejuvenation of the genre. It also won the Best Picture Oscar. The brilliant script by David Peoples—who also wrote *Blade Runner* and *Twelve Monkeys*—marked a major rethinking of the classic American

Western. *Unforgiven* broke with almost every tradition of the standard Western, shooting holes through most audience expectations. And people didn't die cleanly in this movie, they died messily, screaming. The social order of the town of Big Whiskey was held together by corruption, brutality, and drunkenness. The name of the town was significant—Eastwood's film is, among other things, a condemnation of the destructive and corrupting role that alcohol played in the founding of modern America. Eastwood's vision of the Old West was in stark contrast to the classic John Ford model. In *Unforgiven*, there is an implacable worm nibbling away at the moral core of society, while God, and any trappings of religion, is conspicuously absent. In the old days of the Western movie, the church and its preacher were often at the centre of the moral dilemma being played out onscreen. In *Unforgiven*, there is no possibility of salvation; it is every man (or soul) for himself. The town of Big Whiskey is anachronistically secular, more like an old-West Sodom and Gomorrah than the typical Western movie town; it is run with an iron fist by a cruel and corrupt marshal. This same atmosphere reigns in *Appaloosa*.

The film is directed by Ed Harris. A very fine actor, he previously directed *Pollock*, the biopic about American painter Jackson Pollock. *Pollock* was a tremendously powerful and well-crafted film, and Harris' performance as the deeply troubled abstract expressionist was perhaps the best of his career. *Appaloosa* also features Viggo Mortensen, who played opposite Harris in Cronenberg's *A History of Violence*. They had excellent screen chemistry in that one, so it seemed natural that they would team up again. This time around they portray characters on the same side of the moral fence. The screenplay, by Harris and Robert Knott, is based on the novel by Robert Parker. Harris apparently read the novel while on vacation, and was immediately attracted to its screen potential—seeing it as a great buddy movie for him and Viggo Mortensen. Not unlike *Butch Cassidy and the Sundance Kid*, *Appaloosa* is a movie in which friendship plays the role of moral arbiter. The good guys can stretch or ignore the law, and morality, as dictated by religion, is a non-factor; but they cannot transgress the laws of friendship. In the city of Appaloosa, you can cheat on the law and ignore the church, but you can't cheat on a friend because ultimately your life depends on the other's willingness to support you unconditionally.

Set in New Mexico in 1882, the movie is narrated by a man named Everett Hitch (Viggo Mortensen) who tells us that he fought in the Civil War and the Indian Wars, and that for the last twelve years he has been the partner of Virgil Cole (Harris). Together they run a successful "cleaning" business: they rent themselves out to towns that need to clean up their criminal element. They come in as Marshal and Deputy and get rid of the bad guys, with extreme prejudice if necessary. To paraphrase the classic Bacharach-David song (as sung by Gene Pitney), "when it comes to shooting straight and fast, they are mighty good." Appaloosa is a lawless town, run by a rich, powerful outlaw named Randall Bragg (Jeremy Irons). His boys drink the whiskey, use and abuse the ladies of leisure, and take the livestock without paying. Having reached the end of their tether, the town leaders call in Virgil and Everett. Virgil demands (and is given) carte blanche, and faster than you can say "draw!" there are three fresh plots in Boot Hill. Eventually, Virgil and Everett bring Bragg in for the murder of the former marshal. Meanwhile a new woman, an attractive widow, has arrived in town. The "widow lady's" name is Allie French (Renée Zellweger) and she immediately starts making eyes at Virgil. Virgil falls for her, and things get complicated. What, if anything, is this woman up to? Will she possibly cause the breakup of Virgil and Everett's partnership at this most crucial time? Is she a Western Yoko Ono, planting seeds of discord between two friends?

Appaloosa features some stellar art direction and cinematography. The town looks absolutely authentic; a great-looking, Old-West town. The beautiful images are by Aussie Dean Semler who was the Oscar-winning cinematographer on *Dances with Wolves*. There have been several beautifully photographed Western movies in recent years, and *Appaloosa* ranks up there with *The Assassination of Jesse James by the Coward Robert Ford* and *Open Range*. The casting is also excellent. Ed Harris and Viggo Mortensen work very well together and their characters are well written, displaying much dry wit and gently underplayed humorous banter. Ed Harris is the man of action while Viggo is the thinker, and like many intellectuals, he is a bit in awe of someone who can take charge of a touchy situation. Jeremy Irons is very solid as the man we love to hate. His performance reminded me a bit of Daniel Day-Lewis in *There Will Be Blood*, but Irons is more understated and his character a more darkly menacing one than Lewis' quasi-cartoonish villain. We sense that this man would not only "drink your milkshake," but that he would shoot you right between the eyes while drinking it.

Renée Zellweger's performance is more problematical. Zellweger can be a very capable actor in the right role, but there is something very strange about her range of facial expressions (i.e., she has none). I don't want to venture into tabloid journalism, but her face is so expressionless that it looks permanently frozen in a Botox pinch. There has been a lot of Botoxification going on in Hollywood, and while it undoubtedly removes lines and wrinkles, it also makes people look like they are masked. I don't want to start any nasty rumours—I'm much better at spreading rumours than launching them anyway—but from the uniformly blank looks on her face, I would suggest that Renée Zellweger may well be a Botox junkie. She looks like she's been snorting the stuff. The result is that she looks completely phony and artificial. It also occurs to me that Ed Harris may have cast her in this movie for precisely that reason; the character she portrays turns out to be duplicitous, and her lack of expression set off some alarm bells in my head from the git-go.

But to answer the question of whether or not her performance is any good, well, I'm not really sure. I know that sounds completely lame coming from a film reviewer, but I couldn't get past her facial glacier. She delivers her lines convincingly, but there is a strange disconnect about her performance. It is very weird.

In the early going, I thought that *Appaloosa* was full of promise; that it might even be a truly great Western movie. The visuals are gorgeous and the movie wraps itself in a big, beautiful soundtrack that reminded me of *The Big Valley*. I liked the characters, and everything was trotting along nicely (pardner) until Renée Z. showed up and the plot got tangled in its stirrups. The script tries to do too much; the buddy-movie angle and the confrontation with the bad guy would have been plenty for me. Quite simply, the complex love relationship muddies the waters, and the plot piles on enough elements for a TV mini-series. For comparison, in Kevin Costner's *Open Range* — which, by the way, is a much more satisfying viewing experience — the love story enhances the audience's emotional connection without ever losing track of the meat and potatoes of the plot. It also doesn't hurt that Annette Bening, as Costner's love interest, gives a stellar performance. The final twenty minutes of *Appaloosa* are a bit of a let down despite the terrific gunfight near the end that doesn't last as long as it should. Less jawing and more drawing would have been an excellent idea. In a character-driven Western like this, everyone has to be on top of their game and Renée Zellweger is just not strong enough to carry her part of the dramatic load, which is considerable. Western movies are like Horseshoes: *Appaloosa* comes close, but it ain't no ringer.

Balls of Fury

(2007)

Let's name names. I believe that no foul deed should go unpublicized. *Balls of Fury* is directed by Ben Garant and cowritten by Garant and Tom Lennon. You can learn a lot about a person by looking at what they think is funny. For Garant and Lennon, fat people are funny because, well, they're fat; blind people are also funny because they're blind and they bump into things—a lot. Gay men are funny because they scream when they're scared—very loudly. Chinese people are funny because they don't speak English, and blind Chinese people are funnier than anybody.

Balls of Fury makes *Dude, Where's My Car?* look like *Citizen Kane*.

When this movie was conceived (probably at three in the morning, after much libation) I'm sure the writers thought that they hatched an absolutely hilarious idea: a martial-arts movie set in the world of extreme ping pong. What could be funnier?

But what is inspired at three o'clock has usually expired by morning. And don't accuse me of being a snob. I don't mind stupid movies. I don't care if they're stupid, or even terribly politically incorrect. If you think something is funny, and if it makes you laugh, no critic in the world can tell you it's not funny. But there is stupid funny, and then there is just plain stupid.

The acting in *Balls of Fury* is at best annoying and at worst atrocious. No stranger to bizarre performances—have you seen *The Country Bears?*—Christopher Walken as the evil Mr. Feng gives a performance that is extremely bizarre, even by his lofty standards. Still, he comes across as Sir Laurence Olivier in comparison to the rest of the cast. Dan Fogler, cast here as Randy Daytona (former child ping-pong prodigy) tries and tries to breathe humour into the profoundly lame material, but the best that I can say about his performance is that it is trying. The closest the script comes to character development is when Fogler appears in a T-shirt that is two sizes too small.

When the director does not know what to do to keep things moving along (i.e., constantly), he has someone kick someone else in the groin or hit someone with a ping-pong paddle in the groin—or he gets the old blind guy to bump into something. At the end of this movie, I felt like someone had been whacking me across the forehead with a ping-pong paddle for ninety minutes.

Avoid at all costs.

Burn after Reading

(2008)

I call them the "fearless Coens": guerilla filmmakers gleefully taking pot shots at the moral vacuity of modern-day America while revelling in the breathtaking pointlessness and solipsism of human existence. Under the scrutiny of the Coens' lens, America is revealed to be a twisted theme park of greed and stupidity, cruelty and deception; a rollercoaster of perfidy. And the laughter generated by their films (and there is much laughter) is often tinged with hysteria, coloured by the profound absurdity of modern life. Their heroes and heroines are often clueless, petty, and self-centred, but there is also something endearing about them; after all, aren't we all sometimes clueless, petty, and self-centred? Do we not find ourselves to be occasionally adrift, trying desperately to make sense of the senseless, to find clues in what often seems like a clueless universe? I like the Coens. I like them fine. And I like them much more when they fully embrace the absurd, as they do in *Burn after Reading*, than when they embrace nihilism, such as *No Country for Old Men* (see full review further on in this book).

After *No Country for Old Men*, a relentless and unflinching slide into the depths of despair, there was nowhere to go but up. With *Burn after Reading*, the brothers take aim at the intelligence community with a story disguised as a mystery-thriller, overflowing with red herrings, miscommunications, missteps, and misunderstandings. The usual cast of eccentric characters is on parade, with human stupidity splendidly displayed.

The film opens like one of those melodramatic Douglas Sirk films from the fifties, the ones with titles like *Written on the Wind* or *All That Heaven Allows*, with the camera starting from somewhere way up above the clouds (from a spy satellite perhaps) and panning in, down, down, down, into the human world, right into the headquarters of the CIA in Virginia. There we meet CIA analyst Osborne Cox (John Malkovich), a man being demoted because, as his boss tells him flatly, he has "a drinking problem." To this, an outraged Cox responds, "You're a Mormon! Compared to you, everyone has a drinking problem!" He storms out in a huff and quits his job, to the great displeasure of his wife Katie (played by Tilda Swinton, as if she was still playing the Ice Queen in *The Lion, the Witch and the Wardrobe*). We see later that she is perhaps the world's nastiest paediatrician; in a scene where she is treating a young patient, she makes the Wicked Witch of the West seem motherly in comparison. Tilda Swinton is terrific in these kinds of icy, nasty roles — I bet you she gets a lot of dirty looks in the checkout line at the supermarket.

Actually, I can't envision Tilda Swinton standing in a checkout line. There are some actors, larger than life, that I can't imagine just doing normal, everyday things. Just try to imagine Christopher Walken playing Mini-Putt: glaring at the kids and kicking their balls into the grass. Or imagine the looks that Javier Bardem gets when he pulls up to a service station and asks to use the air pump.

So, Tilda Swinton's character, Cox's wife, is having an affair with an ex-secret-service agent named Harry (George Clooney), and Harry is trying to work up the courage to ask his wife for a divorce. Harry spends his spare time surfing the Internet for dates. And one of the women he hooks up with is Linda (Frances Mc-Dormand) who works in a fitness centre. Despite obviously being in excellent shape, Linda is obsessed with her body image; she is convinced that she needs several cosmetic surgery procedures, which she cannot afford and which her insurance refuses to cover. A money-making opportunity seems to present itself when someone at the fitness centre finds a computer disk lying around in a locker. One of the personal trainers, Chad (Brad Pitt), puts it in the computer and gets very excited when he sees what looks like secret CIA files popping up on the screen. Pretty soon Chad and Linda have hatched a half-baked plan to sell these secrets to the

Russians in order to finance Linda's tummy tuck and facelift, not to mention her breast enhancement and liposuction. It (of course) all goes terribly wrong.

The plot of *Burn after Reading* isn't as darkly bizarre as *Fargo*, nor is it as surrealistically superfluous as *The Big Lebowski*, but it does pile on the twists and turns with joyful abandon. By the end, you will identify with the CIA director who says, "well, next time we'll do things differently; if we can only figure out what it is we did!" The alleged plot is really an excuse to give the actors a chance to shine, and shine they do. Some Coens' regulars are onboard, and some newcomers as well. Frances McDormand is terrific, as always, as the depressed fitness instructor desperately seeking love and a facelift. George Clooney, as the amorous three-timing Harry, is a mass of nervous ticks, nervous energy, and bug-eyed paranoia as he becomes more and more convinced that he is being set up for the big fall. John Malkovich is as eccentric and creepy as usual, a character always just a hairpin turn away from going right over the edge. But the revelation of this film is Brad Pitt who portrays McDormand's air-headed accomplice. The scene where he tries to blackmail Malkovich during a late-night phone call is priceless. Those who still doubt that Pitt is a fine actor—he displays astonishing range in this one—are going to get a shock when they see his performance.

Burn after Reading fits snugly into the amoral universe that the Coens have been exploring over the course of a dozen films. Their scripts often seem to be channelling Sir Walter Scott: "Oh what a tangled web we weave, /when first we practice to deceive."

In Coenland, greedy people covet and deceive, but they don't have the brains or the luck to pull off their schemes successfully. They dig themselves into holes and sink deeper and deeper, and oh what fun it is to watch, isn't it? But when we look beyond the silliness, absurdity, and pratfalls, we realize that the portrait of contemporary America is a dark one indeed—a place populated by selfish yahoos mesmerized by their own distorted reflections. The characters in the Coens' films, at least the bad guys or the ones who come to no good, are oblivious to everything but their own desires. This is a vision of America as an immoral carnival of fools where everyone is trying to hustle everyone else—all too blinded by greed and preoccupied with self-gratification to see that the things they think will make them happy are really going to make them miserable. It is a fascinating and disturbing picture of a society that has lost all sense of community, turning its gaze completely inward.

Technology contributes significantly to this erosion of community. Everyone has become so conditioned to communicate by cell phone, Smartphone, and the Internet, that their interpersonal skills seem to have atrophied. By the end of *Burn after Reading* I was reminded of Margie, the pregnant police officer in *Fargo*, saying to the captured killer, "look at all this, what you've done, all this pain and death and destruction. And what for; for some money?"

In the Coens' oeuvre, *Burn after Reading* strikes another resounding blow against idiocy and greed. The final bit of dialogue resonates with Coenesque wisdom:

> **CIA Superior**: What did we learn, Palmer?
> **CIA Officer**: I don't know, sir.
> **CIA Superior**: I don't f****n' know either. I guess we learned, not to do it again.
> **CIA Officer**: Yes, sir.
> **CIA Superior**: I'm f****d if I know what we did.
> **CIA Officer**: Yes, sir. It's, uh, hard to say.
> **CIA Superior**: Jesus F*****g Christ.

'Nuff said?

The Cabin
in the Woods

(2011)

Note: The following review contains numerous spoilers.

The Cabin in the Woods received a certain amount of acclaim from fans for its reinvention of the horror/slasher movie. The director is Drew Goddard who wrote *Cloverfield*, an engaging sci-fi film. He also wrote for the TV series *Lost*, which managed to lose a few viewers along the way. His cowriter and producer is Joss Whedon, who wrote the screenplay for *Toy Story* and also created *Buffy the Vampire Slayer*. That alone would be enough for some, but like Buzz Lightyear, Mr. Whedon is always seeking to go to infinity and beyond. When I heard Whedon describing the plot of *The Cabin in the Woods*, I found his use of the word "therefore" amusing, as in, "a group of college students move into a cabin for a weekend of partying and possibly sex and are therefore dismembered."

You see, horror films are actually fundamentally straight-laced and conservative. Any characters who indulge in sex or drugs (or both) in a slasher-type movie usually have about five minutes of screen time left before they are dispatched with extreme prejudice by the psycho who never had any fun in high school and had no dates and no friends—which is why it drives him totally bat shit to see other young people having sex and smoking dope.

Let's go back to 1939, and more specifically to the publication of the Agatha Christie murder mystery *And Then There Were None*. Some will recall the plot: a group of people has been invited by a mysterious host to spend the weekend on an island off the English Coast where they are systematically murdered in ways that mimic the poem "Ten Little Indians." Those people were not all young, some were old in fact, but they were all accused of having gotten away with murder. The murderer who had gathered them together wanted to exact justice where traditional justice had failed. They were not guiltless.

There are a lot of elements that are presented in the Agatha Christie story that became central to so-called slasher films: an enclosed place (an island, an isolated cabin) from which the characters cannot readily escape, and the sequential murders—part of the fun is guessing who gets it next as they are terminated in ever more creative (and ever gorier) ways. And in slasher films there is often the suggestion (which is often confirmed) that the killer is somehow supernatural or invincible. But how did we get from a series of clever murders of guilty people to gory and perversely imaginative murders of innocent young people?

And the answer is that genre movies survive and thrive in a paradox. On the one hand, they survive by giving audiences exactly what they expect, but they also thrive by surprising the audience and reinventing the rules. The genealogy of the slasher film is fairly straightforward: *Psycho* begat *Texas Chainsaw Massacre* begat *Black Christmas* begat *Halloween* begat *Friday the 13th* begat *Nightmare on Elm St.* begat *April Fool's Day* (which has a plot very similar to *And Then There Were None*) and on and on until we reach *The Cabin in the Woods*. The present film takes all of the conventions of the genre and does two things: squeezes as much blood as it can out of the traditional storylines, and then explodes the conventions to create something new.

When any genre starts to run out of gas (or inspiration—they are sometimes the same thing), it reboots itself by turning into parody. The uninspired genre descends into camp in order to emerge again, transformed. Wes Craven who had done the *Nightmare on Elm St.* pictures came up with *Scream*, a parody of *Halloween* in which the characters become aware that they are in a horror movie. The *Scary Movie* series is cut from the same cloth. But once a genre has passed its parody stage, where can it go?

Postmodern. *The Cabin in the Woods* is a mash-up of different genres, and although not entirely successful—going way over the top at the end—I give it an A for effort. I always hesitate to re-open the never quite closed can of oligochaeta that is the postmodern debate. David Lynch's *Mulholland Drive* is an excellent and entertaining piece of postmodern filmmaking, and interestingly, the cinematographer on *The Cabin in the Woods* is none other than Peter Deming, who was the cinematographer on *Mulholland Drive* and also *Scream 2* and *Scream 3*.

I must now ask the sixty-four million dollar question: why do some audiences get so much enjoyment out of seeing young people get butchered onscreen? Stephen King suggested in his book *Danse Macabre* that horror movies are cathartic—allowing us to confront our worst fears in safety, and giving us the satisfaction of seeing others get it while we escape. That is an oversimplification of what he said, but one of my specialties is oversimplification.

— — —

Plot (with spoilers): Imagine that the five young people going away for what they think will be a party weekend have actually been selected. Selected by whom? Selected by a mysterious government organization that controls everything that will happen in the cabin in the woods. Imagine a very large scientific complex under the cabin. Imagine that every move the kids make is monitored on giant screens, and not only monitored, but influenced by the manipulation of props and by the release of certain substances into the cabin's ventilation system that affects free will.

The Cabin in the Woods answers an age-old question: why do characters in horror movies behave so moronically and so counterintuitively? For example, don't they know that smoking dope and having sex in a horror movie is punishable by death? Don't they know that when one of the creepy yokels warns you about "the old Buckner house" you should listen and avoid the place? Don't they know that if zombies are after you, you shouldn't run in the direction of the cemetery? Don't they know that when things start getting really weird, the group should not split up—thereby making it easier for whoever is trying to kill you to bump you off one at a time?

Under the cabin in the control room, the technicians are releasing psychoactive drugs into the ventilation system, which makes the kids extremely susceptible to suggestion. When a voice whispers, "let's split up" to the star athlete character, he turns to the group and says, "I think we should split up." The kids believe they are acting of their own volition when they make decisions, but actually their free will is being manipulated. They are given choices, but all these choices lead inevitably to death, as when one of the girls unknowingly unleashes the zombie torture family.

Inside the control room, two middle-aged men are calling the shots and getting great, perverse pleasure from watching the kids get slaughtered. Is this sick? The filmmakers would argue that it is no sicker than the perverse pleasure the audience gets from the same spectacle. But I haven't addressed the question of why this is happening.

All of this is happening because the kids are sacrificial lambs. To save the world from the ancient evil gods, every year five young people must be sacrificed in this way. The characters are straight out of Slasher Movie 101: the jock, the blonde bimbo, the intellectual, the stoner, and the nice girl. The cast is good; Chris Hemsworth was an unknown when he was cast in this, and now he is ubiquitous as Thor. Kristen Connolly is not well known but she is a talent deserving of wider recognition. She is bright and tough, and she knows how to treat a zombie.

I've already revealed quite a bit, but I want to say that I didn't like the ending at all—it is way over the top and one of the goriest, splatter-filled scenes ever shot in a horror movie. *The Cabin in the Woods* is rated 18A for disturbing, frightening scenes, extreme violence, gory scenes, offensive language, and sexual content. Bring the family.

Cadillac Records

(2008)

Cadillac Records loosely reimagines the heyday of Chicago's legendary Chess Records. In real life, Chess was founded in 1950 by two Polish immigrant brothers, Phil and Leonard Chess. Strangely, Phil is absent from this movie. Perhaps the idea of having two characters named Chess seemed too confusing—the brothers have been combined into one character, Leonard, portrayed by Adrien Brody. The movie focuses on Leonard and the great blues artists he produced: Muddy Waters, Little Walter, Howlin' Wolf, and Etta James. Movies that celebrate classic blues and the iconic artists who created it are few and far between, so this is exciting for blues fans. But I have good news, and I have bad news.

In the bad news category, I have the same problem with this soundtrack as I have with any movie that doesn't use original recordings. Kevin Spacey didn't do a bad job impersonating Bobby Darin and singing his songs, but to quote Miles Davis, "so what?" When I go to see a movie about Bobby Darin I want to hear Bobby Darin, not Kevin Spacey. And if I'm a Johnny Cash fan, I don't want to hear Joaquin Phoenix. It is reported that Phoenix worked very hard to imitate Cash, and he did an admirable job, but again, what is the point? Still, *Beyond the Sea* and *Walk the Line* were engaging films, and although Spacey was too old to portray the younger Darin he was not miscast. The same cannot be said for Diana Ross as Billie Holiday in *Lady Sings the Blues*. Ross is a fine pop singer, but she was in way over her head portraying Lady Day.

In the case of *Ray*, the Ray Charles biopic with Jamie Foxx, the producers made a very wise decision to have Foxx lip-synch Charles' voice. And Foxx makes it work—there is true artistry

43

in being able to lip-synch convincingly. In *Cadillac Records*, Beyoncé Knowles portrays Etta James and sings James' songs, very credibly I might add. And not only can Beyoncé sing, but she can act. Her performance is electric, alternating between extreme vulnerability and sexual explosiveness; she is a standout. But as good as she is, when I went back and listened to Etta's original recordings, I was stunned to hear how limp these new versions sounded. Beyoncé is not Etta James, and when I boil it all down, I want the real deal. Ultimately, I don't care that Mos Def does a respectable job singing Chuck Berry in this movie—I don't want respectable, I want Chuck.

Of course, all of this is happening because the producers want to repackage the music for a younger audience. They figured—and unfortunately I think they're right—that a soundtrack album full of classic blues and rock-and-roll recordings from the fifties and sixties wouldn't sell. Sad, but true.

Even without the original recordings, *Cadillac Records* offers up some musical highlights. Columbus Short's version of "My Babe" is terrific; full of excitement and swagger. Jeffrey Wright, who is a terrific actor (he was Colin Powell in *W.*), portrays Muddy Waters with great panache, and he also sings like Muddy. His impression of Muddy Waters is one of the best I have ever heard, but it's still an impression. Younger audience members who have never heard the original will be impressed.

When it comes to music that I love, be it blues or pop or jazz, I often just can't help but like certain movies no matter how hokey they are. A case in point is *Grace of My Heart* (1996, dir. Allison Anders) with Illeana Douglas, a wildly fictitious reimagining of the story of Carole King. We all have blind spots, even professional critics, and *Grace of My Heart* is one of those movies that I just can't help enjoying. Yes, it is extremely hokey in places—its vision of West-Coast sixties counterculture is a festival of rose-coloured glasses and tie-dyed clichés—yet it holds up remarkably well to repeated viewings. The soundtrack is a treasure trove of irresistible pop tunes written in the style of Motown, The Beach Boys, and Carole King. The highlight and centrepiece of the film is Douglas' moving and letter-perfect lip-synching of "God Give

Me Strength," an achingly haunting song with lyrics by Elvis Costello and music by Burt Bacharach, beautifully sung by Kristen Vigard.

I am so thrilled that anyone would make a movie in which Willie Dixon's name is even mentioned that I am willing to be extremely indulgent toward *Cadillac Records*. But for all of my enthusiasm, I can't help but note that the script, written by director Darnell Martin, not only pushes the envelope of historical accuracy pretty hard, but positively shreds it to bits in several places. The movie is narrated by the Willie Dixon character—in reality Dixon was the house producer and composer for Chess, and a brilliant musician—but the story contains so many inaccuracies, and so many cheesy Hollywood moments, that it will have serious students of blues history howling. Inevitably it seems (there are few exceptions) when Hollywood portrays the music world or the music business or pop culture in a based-on-a-true-story movie, the audience is served up huge portions of fabrication, if not utter nonsense with tabloid sensibilities spectacularly on display. It is the bane of the musician's existence that Hollywood has been willing to make films about icons like Charlie Parker or Gene Krupa or Chess Records while being totally unwilling to tell it like it really was. Hollywood always needs to distort and amplify, and invent and fabricate, and sentimentalize to the point where an alto sax may well wind up onscreen as a bagpipe. While there may not be any bagpipes in *Cadillac Records*, there also isn't much historical accuracy.

Brody is a great actor, but he seems somehow deflated, projecting little of the passion that the real Leonard Chess had for this music. Chess was a man who went around enthusiastically recording blues artists on Chicago's South Side—a man who bet the farm in order to start a record company dedicated to recording then-unknown Black artists because he believed in their greatness. In contrast to his real-life counterpart, Brody seems almost sedated. He moves slowly and mumbles a lot. There is a lot of mumbling in this movie. Jeffrey Wright, otherwise terrific as Muddy Waters, seems to be going for the Best Achievement in Mumbling nomination. He mumbles his way through certain scenes to the point where some viewers will be wishing for subtitles. Much better is Beyoncé as Etta James. Beyoncé enters the film after about forty-five minutes and things pick up considerably. In her first scene, Leonard Chess discovers Etta's talent in a hotel room when she starts singing in the bathroom.

Reality check.

Etta James may well have sung in a bathroom for somebody, but Leonard Chess didn't discover Etta James; this is pure fantasy. Johnny Otis discovered Etta and she had hits—was an R&B star—before she ever signed with Chess, although she did make many of her classic recordings for the Chess label.

Perhaps you are thinking that no one cares about these details, but I care. At one point, the great but erratic harmonica player Little Walter is shown driving down a country road with Muddy Waters. He spots some musicians in a truck who are passing themselves off as Little Walter and his Jukes, so he gets Muddy to stop the car. He confronts the Little Walter impersonator and shoots the man, right there on the side of the highway.

Reality checkmate.

Little Walter had some severe problems, but why fabricate this outlandish scene and make him out to be a psychotic killer? This never happened. Period.

There is also a lot of nonsense about Leonard Chess saving Etta James' life after a drug overdose. Again, this seems to be a fabrication calculated to inject some pizzazz into the proceedings. And where is Bo Diddley? Where is the mention that Sam Philips in Memphis discovered Howlin' Wolf and told Chess about him? Where is the slightest mention of Ahmad Jamal? We hear that Chuck Berry almost single-handedly made Chess Records rich, but Ahmad Jamal's "Poinciana" was in the charts for 104 weeks and sold a million copies. But you see, Ahmad Jamal was a well-behaved young musician, a serious jazz pianist who neither smoked nor drank; so where is the cinematic value in that? If he did appear in this film, I'm sure the script would have him setting fire to his piano after a drunken binge with Etta and Muddy.

In reality, Leonard Chess did discover Chuck Berry but the movie ignores this most significant event, preferring to dwell on the imaginary discovery of Etta James. By this point the film had become such a fantasy that I would not have been surprised to see hobbits in the recording studio.

If you are a fan of the blues, you are going to want to see this no matter what I say. Some will be greatly disappointed, some will be offended, and others will take it all in stride. And despite all of its numerous faults, *Cadillac Records* is still entertaining, worth seeing for some of the musical numbers and for Beyoncé's performance. And if you want to experience the real Etta James, go to YouTube and check out Etta ranting about Beyoncé's decision to sing Etta's big 1961 hit "At Last" at Obama's inauguration in 2009. Now that rocks.

Clash of the Titans

(2010)

Let me begin with a quote from Tim Burton who had a huge box-office (if not critical) success with *Alice in Wonderland* in 3D. In an interview he stated, "We're surely going to see a lot of bad 3D films in the near future, because Hollywood cannibalizes every recipe for success. That's how the industry works." Well, Tim, the near future is here. I have seen the near future and it is *Clash of the Titans*. And the near future looks like crap.

The original *Clash of the Titans* (1981), as cheesy as it was, was still saved by the work of stop-motion animation master Ray Harryhausen, and the film has attained a kind of cult status. My favourite Harryhausen project remains *Jason and the Argonauts*, a wonderfully entertaining and beautifully crafted film that has been amazing audiences for fifty years. Its painstaking stop-motion effects make many of today's computer-generated histrionics seem artificial and silly in comparison.

The director of the new *Clash of the Titans* is Louis Leterrier, who previously directed *The Incredible Hulk* in 2008 (the version that had Ed Norton looking like Jose Canseco's green cousin). That version was a rethinking of Ang Lee's 2003 *Hulk* starring Eric Bana. It seems that no one liked Lee's version so the studios rebooted it. The term "remake" appears to be passé now; so movies get rebooted. In many cases, the remake proposal should be simply booted out of the meeting, thereby avoiding the painful experience—for the audience—of the reboot. Boot first, and avoid the reboot.

In *Clash of the Titans* we learn that Perseus (Sam Worthington) was rescued as a baby from the sea by the fisherman Spyros. As he grows up, Perseus learns that he is a demigod, the mortal son of the god Zeus (Liam Neeson). The gods have been behaving badly—what else is new?—and the people of Argos are fed up; they have stopped praying. Perseus understands that he is the one destined to put the gods back in their rightful place. With help from a loyal band of brothers, he embarks on a perilous journey to stop Hades (Ralph Fiennes) from raising hell with the monsters he has unleashed on the world. The terrifying beasts include the deadly Medusa, who you will recall has writhing snakes for hair and whose gaze can turn men into stone. Medusa is portrayed here by Russian supermodel Natalia Vodianova, looking absolutely fabulous for a repulsive mythological creature. I wonder who does her snakes; very stylish.

Perseus is helped in his quest by the mysterious Io (Gemma Arterton, who portrayed the sexy Strawberry Fields in the Bond film *Quantum of Solace*).

Note to aspiring producers: When in doubt—and if your budget allows—cast supermodels and Bond girls in key roles. This will distract the males in the audience from noticing the inanities of the script.

The director of this reboot, Louis Leterrier, claims to be a huge fan of the original 1981 version; a terrible irony considering that his version is a monumental mess. *Clash of the Titans* is one of those fake epics that Hollywood often tries to foist upon the unsuspecting public. Watch the trailer and you might think that this is a big, expensive, exciting, action-packed adventure movie.

Nope. In reality, this is a mere $70 million movie—cheap by Hollywood standards for this type of film—masquerading as a $273 million *Avatar*-like blockbuster. *Clash of the Titans* is filled with reheated, regurgitated characters and plot twists. And it looks cheap. Its 3D effects are laughable. The director repeatedly asked Ray Harryhausen to be involved in the film as a creative consultant, but the eighty-nine-year-old Harryhausen refused. God bless you, Ray.

It has always amused me that these so-called epic fantasy films hire great actors to deliver the most insipid dialogue. I read that

Liam Neeson took the role of Zeus because his kids are big fans of Greek mythology. That's ironic because the kids would learn more about Greek mythology from watching those old Hercules cartoons. And why does the movie make Neeson run around in a luminous silver suit looking like he's going to a seventies glam-rock revival party dressed as Freddie Mercury? Don't the other gods *know* that he's number one? The producers could have saved a bundle by casting a lesser actor in this role—you don't need someone as good as Liam Neeson to yell, "Release the Kraken!"

For all of its numerous weaknesses, *Clash of the Titans* is nonetheless educational. I discovered, for example, that the Greek hero Perseus was actually Australian.

You didn't know that either, did you?

Sam Worthington flashes his Aussie accent and portrays Perseus like a kind of hard-nosed, rugby-playing bloke just looking to slay the bloody Kraken, and then it's off to the pub with me mates for a coupla' pints of Faaahster's Laaahger. No worries, mate. Perseus as portrayed by Worthington was such a normal guy that I thought for a minute he might ask Medusa for her phone number.

Tim Burton was right about the rise of the bad 3D movie. The 3D effects in *Clash of the Titans* are the worst I've seen since *Robot Monster* (1953), a film that would be in the Ridiculously Bad B Movie Hall of Fame, if there were such a place. The original poster for *Robot Monster* now sells on eBay for more than the original production budget of the movie. If you suffer from morbid curiosity, you can watch *Robot Monster* on DVD, but not in its original 3D format. It is now only available in "intriguing 2D." Too bad.

The 3D in *Clash of the Titans* is a major distraction. The characters look as if they are trapped in one of those cardboard pop-up children's books. I kept removing my glasses because everything looked so much better without them. By the way, a study conducted at the University of California, Berkeley, found that 3D movies can cause eyestrain along with headaches.

It's incredible how much money is spent on university research projects to prove things that are glaringly obvious to the rest of the population. The strain on the eyes is created because 3D doesn't allow the human eye to follow the rules as the viewer is busy focusing on things both far and near at the same time, possibly resulting in headaches and blurred vision. The study failed to mention that crummy scripts and inept direction often cause the same problems.

Ralph Fiennes as Hades, the evil god of the underworld, seemed to be thoroughly enjoying himself, although it was a bit hard to tell because my vision was blurring so much. It remains a mystery why Hades has such a raspy voice. Is this character development or does Hades spend a lot of time drinking scotch at the Hellfire Bar & Grille? All that warm scotch will do a number on your voice. I can just imagine the preproduction meetings between Fiennes and the director: "I want to do the raspy voice; I'm doing the raspy voice . . . it's in my contract, dammit!"

I hate to make it sound as if *C of the T's* is a complete waste of time, because it isn't. A lot of it is unintentionally funny. And there is actually a good creepy scene featuring some blind witches, but even that isn't original because it is pretty much lifted from *Pan's Labyrinth*. In fact, just about everything in this movie seems to have been lifted from another, better movie: *Star Wars*, *The Lord of the Rings*, and *Jason and the Argonauts*. The incentive of this travesty is not to celebrate Greek mythology or to introduce a younger audience to a classic adventure story; it is to separate the unsuspecting audience from its money. And to add insult to injury, you have to pay a surcharge for the crummy 3D.

They should have called it *Cash of the Titans.*

Contagion

(2011)

There's no season like flu season. *Contagion* is the perfect movie for all you hypochondriacs out there. It will drive you right over the edge. *Contagion* will have you rushing out to buy one of those sanitizing gel dispensers like they have in the hospitals — you know, the ones that are always empty and that the hospital employees never use? Surgical masks also; you are going to need plenty of those. You can just ask your guests to don a surgical mask as they enter the house. Why take chances?

I saw *Contagion* on a Wednesday night at an advance screening in a theatre filled with people, and I wished that the snack bar *had* been selling surgical masks, because there was a guy sitting about three rows behind me and to my left who coughed through the whole movie. And this was not those polite, little dry coughs; this was a big, greasy, hacking cough where it sounds like the person is about to spit up their lungs all over the floor. I turned to my wife after a particularly bad one and said, "I think this guy's going to die before Kate Winslet." At this point in the picture, Kate was wheezing and her skin was a greenish-grey colour.

A big part of the fun in these end-of-the-world movies is trying to guess which character among the all-star cast is going to croak. This morbid guessing game was a big part of the fun of watching *The Poseidon Adventure* back in 1972. I remember how we all sobbed — well, my girlfriend did while I pretended to have something in my eye — when Shelley Winters died saving the others . . . and then they killed off Gene Hackman. Bummer! The original *Night of the Living Dead* ended on a horribly ironic note when the hero was shot after having survived the entire night. Unfortunately in the remake of *War of the Worlds*, they fudged it and Tom Cruise survived.

But in one of my all-time favourite end-of-the-world movies, *On the Beach*, they got it spectacularly right by having everyone die. The Grim Reaper doesn't care if you're Gregory Peck or Ava Gardner or even Fred Astaire, you are checking out. Any movie that can kill off Fred Astaire deserves to be mentioned. I mean, I like Fred Astaire, but my point is that for an apocalyptic film to work, you have to keep the audience guessing about who may be next. You can either have an all-star cast, as *Contagion* does, and try to keep the audience off balance by fearlessly killing off some major stars; or you can make a film like *28 Days Later* with an unknown cast, and then you can really keep the audience on the edge because if you use unknown actors, well, anyone could die—who could know what's going to happen?

Steven Soderbergh, the director of *Contagion*, is not interested in playing games. What he's really interested in is humanity. The scientific elements of the story that relate to the development of the disease are presented with intelligence in a believable way, but Soderbergh is much more interested in pulling the audience into his character's lives and exploring the devastating emotional and psychological impact of a world-wide deadly pandemic on individuals—not to mention the devastating effect on civilization and civilized behaviour.

Soderbergh has made some terrific films, going all the way back to 1989 with *Sex, Lies and Videotape*. Remember when hand-held video recorders were still a novelty and you could build a script around that? Now we have Hollywood stars taking nude pictures of themselves with their cell phones and getting in a snit because the pictures are showing up on the Internet.

Now that's progress.

Soderbergh's second film, *Kafka* with Jeremy Irons, was an amazing expressionistic trip. And more recently *The Informant!* with Matt Damon was a very entertaining bit of sociopolitical satire.

Contagion, sharply written by Scott Burns who also wrote *The Informant!*, doesn't waste any time getting off the ground.

Beth (Gwyneth Paltrow) is sitting in an airport lounge talking to a man on the phone. We quickly understand that they have had a brief affair, and that she is in Chicago on her way home to Minneapolis. She has the sniffles. She looks unwell. Poor Gwyneth, I thought.

I immediately gave her about five minutes of screen time to live. True to form, the script has her keeling over in her kitchen while husband Mitch (Matt Damon) looks on in horror as she falls to the floor foaming at the mouth. Their little son also watches, horrified. She is rushed to the hospital and in no time at all, she is an ex-Gwyneth. Husband Mitch goes ballistic. "What happened to her?" he yells at the doctor. The doctors are noncommittal, "We don't really know [mumble, mumble] . . . maybe meningitis, some people get sick, some don't [mumble]." In the only squirm-inducing scene of the film, we see poor Gwyneth's head being sawed open for the autopsy. Shortly thereafter, her little son is sent home from school with a fever. Would you care to guess what happens next?

Right. He doesn't get to graduate from second grade.

Pretty soon the all-star cast is mobilized. Kate Winslet shows up as Dr. Erin Mears, an epidemic intelligence officer working for Dr. Cheever (Laurence Fishburne) at the Centre for Disease Control (CDC). The clock is ticking as Dr. Erin tries to figure out where the epidemic began. In a bit of a wink-wink to *Sex, Lies and Videotape*, the spread of the disease is pieced together by surveillance footage of the Hong Kong Casino where Beth had spent some time before coming home. As we watch the surveillance video, the waiter coughs, someone touches his glass, the waiter picks it up and hands it to the barman, and someone else touches the bank machine that someone else just sneezed on, and on, and on . . . yuck. No wonder diseases spread so quickly; everyone is inhaling and exhaling everyone else's germs (not to mention assorted bodily secretions, fluids, and whatnot) at breakneck speed. Where is my surgical mask?

The movie has lots of energy, as we hop around from Hong Kong to Chicago to Boston, while the intense soundtrack music keeps us on edge. This is a good, effective soundtrack, and we are also treated to raunchy coughing in glorious Dolby 5.1 surround. Or that may just have been the guy behind me. Anyway, it was loud. We also get big close-ups of colourful graphics of nasty little germs multiplying frenetically, and news reports of more cases, school closures, and transit closures in Chicago.

Meanwhile, back in Minneapolis, Mitch (Damon) discovers that he is immune, and that his teenage daughter may be also. Kate Winslet is risking her life investigating. As the cases multiply, temporary hospitals are set up in hockey arenas. Panic, fuelled by the blogosphere, begins to take hold of the population. Jude Law portrays a conspiracy-theorist blogger who is telling anyone who will listen that the outbreak is actually a ploy cooked up by the pharmaceutical companies. Someone confronts Jude Law and tells him angrily, "you are not a writer; blogging is not writing, it is graffiti with punctuation!"

I hate to criticize a script for being too ambitious when so much of what I see is underdeveloped (and often directed by underachievers), but *Contagion* suffers from an epidemic of subplots. If a tighter focus were placed on the main characters portrayed by Matt Damon, Kate Winslet, Laurence Fishburne, and a few others, we would have more than enough dramatic fodder. But Soderbergh is a victim of his vision. He wants to give us the big picture of these global events spiralling out of control, but in doing so, he scatters his energies. Soderbergh has never been afraid to tackle complex stories—his four-and-a-half-hour epic about Che Guevara was fearless—and ever since his early days with *Sex, Lies and Videotape*, he has been fascinated with communication technology and how information (and in this case disinformation) spreads. In *Contagion*, the spread of the virus mirrors the spread of disinformation and fear on the Internet. It brought to mind the nonsense that was circulating the Internet during the 2009 H1N1 outbreak in Canada. In a very real sense, the script of *Contagion* is not unlike the hyped-up, information-crazed culture that we live in—a fascinating story told in a frazzled and fractured manner that makes it difficult to latch onto the plot's essential elements.

Crazy Heart

and Why Jeff Bridges Is Like Bette Davis

(2009)

There is a famous anecdote, often repeated and perhaps apocryphal, about jazz drummer Buddy Rich being wheeled into the emergency ward after suffering a heart attack. A young attendant asks him, "Mr. Rich, do you have any allergies?" Buddy looks up and replies, "only to country music." On the surface, jazz and country music would seem to mix about as well as oil sands and environmentalists, but there are also many well-confirmed stories about jazz legend Charlie Parker plunking dimes into juke boxes and playing country music songs. When mystified musicians would ask him, "Charlie, what gives?" Bird would answer, "the words are great. Listen to the stories." A good story, whether set to jazz or country music, is always a good story.

Crazy Heart tells a good story.

Jeff Bridges stars and is one of the producers, as is Robert Duvall who has a small but pivotal role in the film. And because movies almost never direct themselves—although both Francis Ford Coppola (*The Godfather*) and Norman Jewison (*In the Heat of the Night*) failed to go home with the Best Director Oscar when their films won Best Picture—let's take note that *Crazy Heart* is the work of a rookie director, thirty-eight-year-old Scott Cooper.

The creative combination of Cooper and Bridges yields spectacular results as Bridges gives a remarkable performance as the broken down, alcoholic country singer "Bad" Blake.

When a director works with an actor of the calibre of Jeff Bridges, he has to know when to let him go and when to gently reel him in, or hold him back. The problem is that great actors are often more like forces of nature than human beings, and it is exceedingly difficult (read: impossible) to hold back a hurricane or a tidal wave. Jack Nicholson immediately springs to mind as someone who has chewed up some world-class directors and spit out their bones after giving completely over-the-top performances. Even a genius like Stanley Kubrick could not contain Nicholson in *The Shining*, and what could have been not only a great horror movie but one of the great movies of the period was almost reduced to rubble by Nicholson's histrionics. There are many, many examples of movies being trashed by excessive acting, particularly when the script calls for extensive substance abuse and drunken behaviour—but I am very happy to say that Bridges, true to form, underplays the role of the alcoholic Blake and allows the man's humanity to shine through.

Jeff Bridges is cut from the same acting cloth as Humphrey Bogart and Bette Davis. In an era when many of their peers overplayed for the camera, they opted for understatement, giving the camera just enough so that the audience could fill in the blanks and round out the character. Of course, sometimes histrionics are exactly what is called for, and Bette Davis in particular never had any problems on that front (see *What Ever Happened to Baby Jane?*), but she never let the dramatic fireworks overwhelm the character. Even when Bridges is playing outrageous, almost cartoonish characters as he does in *The Big Lebowski* or *The Men Who Stare at Goats*, there is always something completely believable and endearing about his characterizations.

The tagline to *Crazy Heart* is that "Bad" Blake is a broken-down, hard-living country music singer who's had way too many marriages, far too many years on the road, and one too many drinks way too many times.

Sound way too predictable?

This could be the Johnny Cash story or the Hank Williams story or a remake of *Tender Mercies* (i.e., talented singer hits the bottle and hits rock bottom, but in the end is saved by the love of a good woman and a bible). But even though *Crazy Heart* does explore those well-worn story elements, there is more to the narrative than we expect.

"Bad" Blake (Bad is his stage name; "I was born bad," he is fond of saying) used to be a star, and he still has a loyal and devoted following. As the movie opens, Bad arrives at his next gig somewhere in New Mexico in his battered 1970s Chevy truck. Staring incredulously at the sign, he realizes that his long-time manager has booked him to play a bowling alley. It may be a bowling alley with a bar, but it is still a bowling alley; it ain't The Horseshoe Tavern. I smiled when I saw this because I thought it was a little nod to the ubiquitous bowling in *The Big Lebowski*. I also smiled because as an unknown musician, I once actually played a bowling alley. Of course playing a bowling alley when you're on your way up is something quite different from playing it when you're fifty-seven and on your way down with, if you'll excuse the pun, one foot in the gutter. But Bad is a trooper so he makes the best of it, and we see that he is still a dynamic performer with a loyal fan base. He is also still able to pick up star-struck women, although I have to say that the pickup in high heels looked almost as road weary as the pickup in the parking lot.

I'm not a musical snob—I'm a film reviewer, dammit!—but I am also not a fan of country music. I was a bit concerned that this would distance me from the film. I do, however, subscribe to Duke Ellington's philosophy that there are two kinds of music, "good music and the other kind." When I saw that T-Bone Burnett was the musical producer, my fears evaporated; anyone nicknamed T-Bone has to be real good or they would never live it down. This man has worked with and produced records by B.B. King, Tony Bennett, Elvis Costello, and Bob Dylan. The songs he has written for *Crazy Heart* (co-composed with the late Stephen Bruton) constitute a crafty blend of all of the best elements found in country music: gospel, blues, and zydeco. The soundtrack elevates the film considerably.

Jeff Bridges does his own singing and gives credible performances, very wisely avoiding the dreaded nasal twang. He's not a great singer, but how many great country singers are there? I mean, once you've heard Ray Charles sing "I Can't Stop Loving You," you can pretty well die and go to the great bowling alley in the sky; it's never gonna be any better. The songs in the movie have titles like "I Don't Know" and "Fallin' Feels like Flying," avoiding the equally dreaded gimmicky country song titles like "The Beer I Had for Breakfast Is Coming Back for Lunch"—although given the character's extreme alcoholism, this would actually have been quite appropriate. One song that Bridges sings has the convoluted title "I Used to Be Somebody but now I'm Somebody Else"; it actually makes sense if you think about it.

Maggie Gyllenhaal portrays Jean, a young journalist who interviews our hero and winds up in a complicated relationship with Bad; this is further complicated by the fact that she has a young son. Gyllenhaal is very good. She has an expressive face and when things start heating up between her and Bad, we can see her thinking, "don't get involved with this guy, he is going to let you down and he is no father figure—he is a drunk." One glance at Bad's track record should be enough to scare her off: the man has been married four times and has a twenty-eight-year-old son who he hasn't seen in twenty-four years. He is not perhaps ideal dad material. But in the time-honoured tradition of the best and most sentimental country music songs, perhaps the love of a good woman can save old Bad from himself after all. People can change, can't they?

The solid script mostly avoids the genre clichés, and the film never feels overly contrived. There is strong chemistry between Gyllenhaal and Bridges; the emotions are palpable. Some viewers may quibble with the dénouement because (without giving anything away) in wanting to avoid cliché endings, the script has fabricated one that is not completely satisfying. Well, sometimes life imitates country music, and sometimes there just aren't any happy endings because life is more Johnny Cash than Barry Manilow.

"Bad" Blake is one of Jeff Bridges' strongest performances, and it is refreshing to see a Hollywood movie where nobody rides a dragon, nothing blows up, nobody has blue skin, it's not in 3D, and nothing sinks, gets teleported, or shot into space. *Crazy Heart* is basic, quality filmmaking: an engaging story with believable (and likeable) characters we care about. What a concept. Is this modern?

The Dark Knight Rises

(2012)

I have endeavoured over the years to connect the film I am reviewing with its social and political context in order to give the listener (or reader) a sense of how a particular movie fits as a cultural artifact—to explore what it may or may not reveal about the broader social milieu that spawned it. The premiere of *The Dark Knight Rises* in July 2012 coincided with a horrific mass shooting at a movie theatre in Aurora, Colorado. I do not want this review to focus on that tragic event, nor do I wish to use this review as a springboard for a sociopolitical rant on the insanity of making high-powered assault rifles and all kinds of weaponry as easy to purchase as lawnmowers and snow tires. That being said, in the wake of the killings in Colorado, *The Dark Knight Rises* has pundits on both sides of the American political spectrum standing on their soapboxes.

It seems that almost everyone is reading some kind of subtext into the storyline. If we go back to 2005 and *Star Wars: Episode III Revenge of the Sith*, we might recall that the political right in the United States was in a major snit about a line of dialogue from the film, when the evil Anakin says to Obi-Won, "If you aren't with us, you are the enemy." For some wild and unfathomable reason, some interpreted that as being a reference to George Dubya's infamous post-9/11 comment, "If you're not with us, you're with the terrorists." George Lucas' subsequent denials notwithstanding, it was hard not to see his dialogue as political allegory writ large. In *The Dark Knight Rises*, and despite Rush Limbaugh's excitable and sweeping pronouncements, things are a little more complicated.

By the way, doesn't the name Rush Limbaugh sound like the name of a stinky cheese? "I'll have three hundred grams of that Rush Limbaugh, please. Is it runny?"

Among Limbaugh's many claims concerning *The Dark Knight Rises*, his statement that the name of the villain, Bane, is a reference to presidential candidate Mitt Romney's former company, Bain Capital, is way off the mark. Yes, Limbaugh is yet again misinformed. The character of Bane was created in 1993 well before Mitt Romney had any political aspirations. And anyway, the evil guy is B-a-n-e and the evil company is B-a-i-n, so not only is Limbaugh a stinky cheese, but he is a cheese that can't spell, which is the worst kind.

The Dark Knight Rises is not so much a movie as a two hour and forty minute force of nature, a veritable cinematic hurricane. I saw it in IMAX and found some scenes a bit overwhelming. This has to be the loudest movie I have ever seen. I felt like I was caught in a windstorm. To make matters worse, the score is the equivalent of musical TNT, and Batman speaks in a raspy voice just above a whisper while Bane has a mask over his face, which muffles his voice. I missed every three words of dialogue. When it was all over, my brain felt like it had just been run through the car wash with the top down.

This is Hollywood filmmaking on a monumental scale. About an hour is shot in IMAX, and the aerial scenes are spectacular. This is a $250 million movie that looks like it cost $250 million, but the sound and the music are way over the top. Older viewers may want to turn down their hearing aids for this one, or even leave them at home altogether.

Even though it is the third and final instalment of a trilogy, *The Dark Knight Rises* works quite well as a standalone piece. Viewers who missed the first two will not be terribly confused. The story takes place eight years after the events depicted in *The Dark Knight*. You will recall that Batman (Christian Bale) took the rap for DA Harvey Dent's death. Dent was the evil Two-Face, and Commissioner Gordon (the always superb Gary Oldman) had persuaded Batman to take the blame in order to pass a new tough anti-crime law.

As our story begins, Bruce Wayne has become a recluse à la Howard Hughes with only faithful Alfred as company. But Wayne starts to emerge from his cocoon when a sexy cat burglar named Selena Kyle (Anne Hathaway) steals his mother's pearl necklace. Meanwhile the evil and psychotic Bane, a mass of muscles who wears what looks like a round gas mask, kidnaps a Russian scientist in spectacular fashion from a plane in flight. This aerial assault is an amazing piece of cinema: one plane overtakes another and mercenaries shimmy down ropes to enter the plane containing the Russian scientist. It's all very spectacular and of course, if you give it any thought, it's all supremely silly. After this incredible in-flight kidnapping, my wife turned to me and said, "Wow, was that ever complicated. Why didn't they just kidnap the scientist before he got on the plane?"

I never know what to say when I'm faced with that kind of implacable logic. If my wife was a supervillain bent on world domination, Batman wouldn't stand a chance.

Many of the comments from political axe grinders like ole' Rush focus on a midday attack launched by Bane and his minions on the New York Stock Exchange—while holding everyone hostage, they take over the computers and make a gazillion trades that displace incredible amounts of money into secret accounts. The question that some pundits have been asking is this: is the movie equating the Occupy Wall Street movement with Bane's terrorist attack? After all, much of the plot revolves around class warfare. Bane presents himself as the liberator of the people, declaring that "the rich have gone too far; they are living too high and they must be brought down." Bane is of course nothing of the sort; he is a fascistic character intent on destroying Gotham and everyone in it. But his actions kick-start a kind of revolution that allows the masses—a wild-eyed mob would be more to the point—to invade the apartments and dwellings of the wealthy class and to loot and destroy and essentially turn everything upside down. While this social upheaval is going on, most of the Gotham police force is trapped underground, powerless to intervene. Batman, after a rough first encounter with Bane, finds himself held prisoner in a hellish prison somewhere (we think) in the Middle East. Things get very grim indeed before the dawn finally arrives.

I think that the comparisons to the Occupy Wall Street (OWS) movement are overly simplistic, if inevitable. For beginners, OWS was a grassroots movement born out of social networking and genuine grassroots anger at economic injustice and inequity. OWS was not a violent movement, and it did not aim to destroy the rich. That being said, *The Dark Knight Rises* offers an unequivocally negative vision of what happens when the rich are removed from the equation—without the rich running things, society quickly falls apart. Gotham is saved in extremis by the enlightened billionaire Wayne and superior military technology. The good (and not so good) citizens of Gotham are unable to organize themselves into an effective force for change; a superhero is needed because the forces of evil are too overwhelming.

It's not a coincidence that superhero movies are hugely popular right now as many people feel like hostages to shadowy and inscrutable economic forces that seem to invariably place profit ahead of people. Any recent opinion poll will confirm that the population at large does not believe that governments can solve the big problems; many in fact believe that governments are increasingly *part* of the problem. In 2012 American voters had to choose between Obama and Romney, but I suspect that the candidate of choice for many voters would have been Batman, and why not? He is a much sharper dresser.

The Dark Knight Rises is a thrill ride, an atomic blast of a movie. And it is also very dark. If you are looking for escapism, you may feel that the story arc is too closely informed by today's grim headlines—and you may find yourself wondering if this is really your idea of entertainment. The movie is spectacular, exciting, brutal, and loud. It is a product of the often depressing, angst-ridden times in which we live. It is miles removed from the sensibilities that coloured, once upon a time, the superhero movies of my youth. The Dark Knight does indeed rise (to the occasion) but only after he has been beaten, brutalized, and defeated; thrown into a hole from which there seems to be no escape; left in the dark to confront his own personal demons. This may be art, but where is the fun?

I miss Adam West. Or maybe I really just miss my nine-year-old self watching Adam West on that wonderful, goofy program. Anyway, I miss something. Farewell, oh Batman of my youth . . .

The cast of *The Dark Knight Rises* is first-rate, and Anne Hathaway as Catwoman not only steals the show, but saves it. She is a visual treat, and is also a desperately needed beacon of levity in the darkness. I will venture to say that without her witty asides and obvious sense of fun, the whole exercise would have been (for me) just about unwatchable. Michael Caine as Alfred the ever-faithful butler is very moving in a couple of scenes. The English actor who portrays Bane is Tom Hardy. This young man has serious acting chops—he won a Laurence Olivier award for his stage work in London—but what can you do with a leather gas mask on your face? It's a bit like trying to do card tricks while wearing oven mitts. I missed quite a lot of his dialogue, but his imposing presence and body language still managed to generate onscreen menace.

The Dark Knight Rises is a monumental film, and even at almost three hours it never drags. A thrill ride, certainly, but before you drag the kiddies out to experience it, be aware that it is a very dark and violent thrill ride.

The Day the Earth Caught Fire

Classic Film Review

(1961)

Editor: I don't care a tinker's damn about this eclipse of the sun as such; the evening papers will cane it, it'll be dead by tomorrow morning. But what I do care about is why there was an eclipse of the sun ten days before it was due. Bill, this is your department.

Bill Maguire: I don't know why everybody regards me as Nostradamus. Your guess is as good as mine.

Editor: Yes, but I don't want guesses, I want facts. Try someone on top. Sir John Kelly. (Britain's Chief Meteorologist)

Bill Maguire: Stenning got in to see Kelly.

Peter Stenning: He had twenty-eight armed guards around him.

Editor: Yes, but what did he say?

Peter Stenning: He wouldn't even say goodnight in case it was taken as an official comment on the future of mankind.

Editor: Which convinces me even more that information is being withheld in Downing Street.

Long before anyone ever began worrying about global warming and climate change there was *The Day the Earth Caught Fire* (1961, dir. Val Guest), a superior end-of-the-world movie enhanced by an almost *cinéma vérité* feel, excellent performances, and an intelligent, engaging script written by director Guest and Wolf Mankowitz. In 1962 the script won the award for Best British Screenplay given by the British Academy of Film and Television Arts. If you haven't seen this movie—and if you are perhaps skeptical of the sensational title or of the rather cheesy DVD cover art—allow me to reassure you that *The Day the Earth Caught Fire* is arguably the best end-of-the-world movie ever made. I say arguably because when we are talking about movies of very high quality, the whole question of "the best" becomes open to interpretation. For an end-of-the-world movie to be truly effective, it is not necessary to show mountains collapsing or tidal waves razing New York City. What you really need is a superior script and sympathetic, believable characters. This one has both.

The film is almost entirely character driven (i.e., there are no monsters, no flying saucers, and no razzle dazzle). It is a sci-fi film made for adults, about adults, and it is riveting from beginning to end. That is a rare tour de force for a sci-fi movie that has almost no special effects and takes a full hour of its ninety-nine minute running time to completely reveal the details of its doomsday scenario. Director Val Guest not only knew how to make the most of a limited budget—the film was made for about £200,000 ($800,000)—but he was also an expert at building suspense.

— — —

The more you can suggest in a film, and not show, the better.
—Val Guest

When discussing a movie that has everything going for it, it is sometimes difficult to know where to begin. The first thing that attracted me to *The Day the Earth Caught Fire* was the presence of Janet Munro, a wonderfully charismatic and versatile actress. I first saw a Janet Munro film at the Regent Theatre in Ottawa when I was seven years old. She starred in a Disney movie titled *Darby O'Gill and the Little People* (1959, dir. Robert Stevenson). It was an exceptionally entertaining family picture that still evokes fond memories today, and it left me more than a little smitten with Ms. Munro.

In *The Day the Earth Caught Fire*, Munro took on her first adult role. She was then twenty-six and had just left Disney Studios where she had been hugely successful portraying high-spirited adolescents. Here she portrays Jeannie, a bright, confident young woman who is employed as a secretary in the Met Office, the British Meteorological Service. Munro's performance is as convincing for its lack of artifice as it is endearing for its emotional honesty. The film stars Edward Judd as reporter Peter Stenning. Already a popular television personality in Britain, this was Judd's first big-screen role and he is excellent as the emotionally wounded, cynical reporter going through a difficult custody battle for his young son. His newspaper career increasingly in jeopardy because of his drinking, Peter falls under the positive spell of Munro's Jeannie and starts to turn his life around just as the earth faces disaster as a consequence of two extremely ill-advised atomic tests conducted simultaneously by the United States and the Soviet Union. Whereas the vast majority of sci-fi films (even today) are exclusively plot driven (i.e., first *this* happens, then *that* happens, and so on to the conclusion), *The Day the Earth Caught Fire* is a rare and refreshing viewing experience because it allows for character development—we feel involved because we believe and identify with these characters submerged in an increasingly desperate situation. And for the first hour or so, the film's central plotline focuses on the investigative journalism that eventually reveals the truth about the imminent cataclysm facing mankind. By this point, the film's gritty realism and attention to detail have left no room for doubt in the viewer's mind. The drama of an end-of-the-world movie isn't generated by Bruce Willis yelling, "We are down to our last drill bit!" or Dennis Quaid snowshoeing across a frozen Times Square, it is generated by a thoughtful script that takes the time to develop its characters, and allows the audience to step inside their shoes and share the mind-boggling, heart-thumping reality of being on the very edge of oblivion.

It is of course great fun if a movie can show you convincing scenes of mass destruction, but it isn't necessary. What is necessary, however, is that we are presented with a cast of believable and likeable characters. We must be able to identify with the people onscreen, and we must share their fears and apprehensions. The main reason that *The Day the Earth Caught Fire* works so beautifully is that Jeannie, Peter, and Bill (Leo McKern) are flesh and blood characters: flawed, sympathetic, with personal lives and personal concerns. The profound tragedy of the impending disaster is played out on a very personal level. Just as Peter and Jeannie have finally discovered love, the whole world is about to go up in flames. And as would be the case in real life, they can't help but take it personally. For Peter, divorced and increasingly alienated from his young son, the imminent end of the world appears as a bad joke of cosmic proportions—the catastrophic, collective dénouement of everything that has gone wrong with his life.

When faced with the challenge of presenting an unbelievable story, the wisest directors adopt a matter-of-fact approach. This is the path Robert Wise followed for *The Day the Earth Stood Still* in 1951, and it is also the approach Guest adopted for *The Day the Earth Caught Fire* a decade later. Both films wrap their extraordinary subject matter in a quasi-documentary style. In Wise's film, real television reporters of the day like Drew Pearson were cast and are seen commenting on the unfolding events. By similar design, Guest cast a recently retired *Daily Express* editor, Arthur Christiansen, to portray (who else?) the editor of the *Daily Express*, the paper that eventually breaks the story that the earth has been pushed off its orbit by dual atomic tests and is spinning toward the sun. Christiansen was a legendary newspaper figure, and despite his limited acting abilities—by all accounts he had trouble remembering his lines—his colourful personality and in-depth knowledge of newspaper procedure and jargon lend much credibility to the unfolding events. To add even more realism, the sets constructed for the film were an exact replica of the actual *Daily Express* offices of the time.

The Day the Earth Caught Fire also makes very effective use of archival news footage of various natural and man-made disasters. Brilliant use of library footage—seamlessly integrated with studio footage—gives the viewer a believable image of cataclysmic weather changes brought about by the earth's orbital shift. When the earth has begun to get closer to the sun and a devastating heat wave settles on England causing most of the water in the Thames to evaporate, the film smartly incorporates impressive library footage of the massive fires that were unleashed by German bombings in WWII. Interestingly, director Guest actually served as a volunteer fireman in London during the blitz.

In *The Day the Earth Stood Still*, Robert Wise made very effective use of Bernard Hermann's memorable Theremin score. In *The Day the Earth Caught Fire*, Val Guest decided against using any background music at all. He felt, and rightly so, that this extraordinary story would appear more realistic to audiences without a musical soundtrack, and so the only music included is source music (music that originates from a source on the screen, like a radio, for example). To further heighten the film's realism, and to duplicate the electric atmosphere of a big-city newsroom, Guest included much overlapping dialogue. The use of this technique transforms the film's soundscape into a trove of verbal riches: ironic asides, muttered cynicisms, and colourful non sequiturs. In fact, the film would remain effective and enjoyable on the strength of its soundtrack alone. Overlapping dialogue had also previously been used to superb effect in Howard Hawks' sci-fi film classic *The Thing from Another World* (1951).

Both Wise and Guest shot their films entirely in black and white — except for the orange-tinted film stock used to suggest unbearable heat in the framing scenes at the beginning and end of *The Day the Earth Caught Fire*. Working with a much larger budget than the one at Guest's disposal, Wise certainly could have opted to make *The Day the Earth Stood Still* in colour. But he rightly judged that black and white would more effectively create the ambience of realism, mimicking the familiar newsreels of the day, and he believed this to be of paramount importance if audiences were to buy the fantastic storyline.

The Day the Earth Caught Fire benefits enormously from Harry Waxman's razor sharp cinematography, and the use of Panavision makes the movie a real treat, communicating to the viewer a particularly rich visualization of the ever-bustling newsroom and the increasingly transformed and chaotic London environment. The film paints such a realistic portrait of a big-city newspaper, complete with widescreen shots of giant printing presses, that it could be reedited without the sci-fi story elements and used as a short educational film about the inner workings of a large newspaper, circa 1960.

Although the film relies very little on special effects, it still features some first-rate instances of visual trickery, thanks to the expertise of legendary special-effects artist Les Bowie. Born in Vancouver in 1913, Bowie had a long and storied career at Hammer Films and American International where his talent and imagination considerably elevated the production values of many low-budget Roger Corman films.[2]

Les Bowie is credited with inventing the "glass shot"—a method of painting additional scenery on a pane of clear glass, which is then placed in front of the camera. Using this inexpensive method, it is possible to effectively transform even the most mundane sets into extraordinary decor. Bowie was a painter of rare skill, and the combined use of his realistic matte paintings with the "glass shot" technique allowed even modestly budgeted films to present audiences with wondrous vistas. In *The Day the Earth Caught Fire*, his photographic effects of the eerie fog that envelops London and the images he created of a dried-out Thames are convincing and add much to the film's verisimilitude. In the sixties and seventies, Bowie worked on numerous films, including Kubrick's *2001: A Space Odyssey*, where he was credited as special-effects supervisor. He was also part of the special-effects team that won an Academy Award for *Superman* (1978, dir. Richard Donner). He died in 1979.

If you are a fan of sci-fi or simply a movie buff, you have to see *The Day the Earth Caught Fire*. It is a glowing example of the magic that can be created when the budget (as modest as it may be) is channelled intelligently, placing the emphasis on storytelling instead of splash.

---

2   Note: The phrase "low-budget Roger Corman films" is obviously redundant. Sorry.

Déjà Vu

Time Travel

(2006)

In the old days, characters in time-travel stories wanted to visit the future because the future was going to be so darned wonderful.

Remember *that* future? People were going to have tons of leisure time, and we would spend our days frolicking in a world devoid of hunger; a lush, green place where war was only a distant memory. Yes, the future was going to be great. And if man had really evolved, well, perhaps even telemarketing might be outlawed, and humanity would truly be free to pursue higher interests rather than spending its time answering the phone. Nowadays, I doubt that many of us would even want to visit the future. As Yogi Berra famously said, "the future ain't what it used to be." In fact, it seems that just the mention of the word "future" fills us with dread in a way that H.G. Wells never imagined back in the 19th century when he wrote *The Time Machine*. I'll bet that if you asked fifty people what they would do with a time machine, almost all of them would say they'd want to travel back to the past, to some quiet era where life is simpler, gentler, more civilized—a time before anyone had ever heard of greenhouse gas emissions and harmonized sales tax.

World-renowned physicist Stephen Hawking, while not altogether dismissing the concept of forward time travel, has expressed profound skepticism about the feasibility of travelling back in time. According to Hawking, the absence of tourists from the future supports the idea that backward time travel isn't possible.

With all due respect, I disagree.

The apparent absence of tourists from the future may only prove that:

a) They are here, but have enough sense to keep a low profile; or

b) They have enough sense not to visit this particular era at all. I mean, if you're going to spend a pile of money on a time-travel vacation, you at least want to go somewhere that's clean and quiet and where the people are polite. Above all, you want to visit a place that's safe (i.e., where people don't drive SUVs while talking on their cell phones or tweeting their friends on their Smartphones).

— — —

In time-travel stories, the traveller is often motivated by the desire to change something in the past, usually an event of major international importance. In real life, we all have events in our lives that we would like to change—or wish had never happened. Generally, in sci-fi films, time machines are used to address big issues, not to go back in time to warn yourself not to attend that office Christmas party in 1988 when you got drunk and flirted with the boss's wife (and found a pink slip on your desk the next afternoon when you finally stumbled into work with a wicked hangover).

Usually the event focused on by the time traveller is something a bit less frivolous. Not that losing your job isn't important, but it probably isn't going to change the course of world history, unless you're the president of the United States and the reason you've lost your job is because someone has put a bullet through your brain. Indeed, I'm sure that many people have fantasized about travelling back in time to prevent JFK or Martin Luther King or RFK or John Lennon from being assassinated.

If you are a Montréal Expos fan, perhaps you sometimes fantasize about journeying back in time to prevent Expos manager Jim Fanning from calling in Steve Rogers to pitch to Dodger Rick Monday in the ninth inning of the deciding game five of the 1981 National League Championship Series. Of course, given the mental makeup of many baseball managers (i.e., it's my way or no way), it seems unlikely that even a time traveller equipped with a video of Monday's ensuing home run could dissuade Fanning from putting Rogers into the game at that fateful moment. As for Red Sox fans, well, forget it. They have so many of these historical disasters to contend with—1946, 1975, 1978, 1986, 2003—that the gyroscopic stabilizers on their time machines would have a meltdown, and they'd never be able to find their bearings.

— — —

Even if the time travellers' intentions are good, things might go horribly wrong. Say, for example, that you have a time machine, and your plan is to keep Bobby Kennedy from being assassinated. A little after midnight on June 5, 1968, you hide in the pantry of the Ambassador Hotel in Los Angeles, and just when Sirhan B. Sirhan comes up behind the Senator, you push the would-be assassin away. But what if the gun still goes off?

And what if, instead of killing RFK, the stray bullet strikes a bystander? And what if the victim turns out to be your own father? Fatally wounded, he now dies while still a bachelor, and the result is that you will never be born.

Congratulations! You have just saved Bobby Kennedy, but you have also just erased yourself from existence.

But here comes the time-travel paradox: by saving Bobby you have inadvertently killed your own father, and you will never be born. But if that is the case, then you didn't exist to go back in time in the first place, so your father will *not* be killed and you *will* be born. This is a slightly modified version of a time-travel paradox originally posited by writer René Barjavel in his book *Le voyageur imprudent* (The Imprudent Traveller, 1943).

— — —

I like Denzel Washington—although not in the Facebook way—or rather I like the characters he usually portrays, the glaring exception being Frank Lucas in *American Gangster*. But usually, his characters are forthright, honest, tough but fair, and rather noble but not aloof; men who have the courage to put themselves on the line for what they believe in. I find that he gives consistently solid performances even when the movie is not great. Washington does a good job here working with director Tony Scott, who he previously worked with on *Crimson Tide*, a movie that was not only not great, but should have been torpedoed in the development stage. Tony Scott has a very spotty record; he directed *Days of Thunder* with Tom Cruise—a formulaic vehicle that managed to make NASCAR racing seem even more mind-numbingly boring than it really is. He also directed *The Fan*. For more about that bomb, refer to "The worst baseball movie of all time?" in this book.

If the director of *Déjà Vu* has a spotty record, what about producer Jerry Bruckheimer? This is the man who gave us *Pearl Harbor* and *Armageddon*. Here's an attractive time-travel fantasy: get in a time machine, and prevent Bruckheimer from making *Pearl Harbor*, thereby saving everyone three and a half hours of their lives.

Déjà Vu begins in New Orleans on Mardi Gras as a ferry filled with families leaves the dock for a festive cruise. A few minutes into the journey, a series of horrific explosions rip the ferry apart, resulting in great loss of life. Enter our hero, Agent Doug Carlin (Denzel Washington), a special investigator for the ATF (Alcohol, Tobacco and Firearms). In no time at all, Agent Doug has gathered irrefutable evidence that this explosion was a terrorist act. Almost as quickly, he is approached to join a secret team of investigators who are using new, cutting-edge surveillance technology to solve the crime.

Bodies are washing up on the shore, and it's all quite horrific. Strangely, one of the bodies is of a young black woman who was killed a few hours before the explosion and placed there to make it appear as if she was on the ferry. It is this murder that becomes the prime focus of our hero's investigation. He becomes convinced that this woman was killed by the terrorist who blew up the ferry. "Solve this murder," he says, "and you solve the whole thing." The cutting-edge surveillance technology that I mentioned allows the investigators to look back into the past, but only exactly four days and six hours ago.

Why only four days and six hours, you ask?

The easy answer is because the writer says so. This is one of those totally contrived, sci-fi plot elements that cannot be logically explained. Or perhaps it allows our hero to spy on the young attractive murder victim for four days, and to slowly fall in love with her as he sees her going about her life leading up to her murder. The investigators hope that she will lead them to the terrorist because they know that she met him at some point. Soon, our hero's obsession with the young woman grows, and he starts to think that maybe the past can be altered and that she can be prevented from dying, thereby also preventing the ferry from exploding. We are now introduced to a key time-travel plot element: that annoying quirk that makes it impossible to change the past. No matter how hard you try, the event you're trying to change or prevent always winds up happening anyway, except that there may also be unfortunate rebounds from your actions, and you may mess up the present.

In this case, our hero discovers that he can send a note back in time to himself, four days ago, to tell himself where the terrorist will be the night before he plants the bomb. But here comes the Fanning Effect: the note winds up in his partner's hands, and his partner winds up getting killed. Worse, now the terrorist needs a new vehicle to plant the bomb — the vehicle he had originally used is no longer an option — so the young woman is now in peril as it will be her vehicle that will be stolen after she is murdered. Would she have died if the good guys hadn't tried to change the past?

So, our hero Agent Doug decides to go back in time in order to fix all of this. One of the best lines comes when he is getting ready to be zapped back in time, and the technician tells him, "you don't have to do this," to which he answers "maybe I already have." I smiled when I heard this. This is exactly the kind of spiffy time-travel dialogue I enjoy; kudos to writers Bill Marsilii and Terry Rossio.

Denzel Washington seems to be one of those rarest of rare birds: film actors who seem absolutely incapable of giving a less than excellent performance, no matter what material they are handed. He is in fine form here. Val Kilmer is also very good as the head of the secret investigation team. Jim Caviezel as the domestic terrorist—a Timothy McVeigh type of psycho—is suitably creepy.

The choice of New Orleans as the setting is excellent. The city has a lot of atmosphere, although I was shocked by some of the damage. At one point, the terrorist is hiding out somewhere in a neighbourhood that was devastated by Katrina, and it looks like it happened yesterday. I think the producers wanted to make a statement—in fact, the movie is dedicated to the spirit and the people of New Orleans—and the production had actually started before Katrina hit, so it was held up, but the producers absolutely wanted to do it in New Orleans. Dialogue referring to the Katrina disaster was added later to make the script more timely.

Déjà Vu is a tight, intelligent thriller. It kept me involved and guessing, and I found the time paradoxes sharp and entertaining. This is one of the better science-fiction thrillers of the past several years, and I look forward to going back in time at some later date and watching it again for the first time . . .

The Fan

The Worst Baseball Movie
of All Time?

(1996)

The Fan (dir. Tony Scott) stars Robert De Niro as a demented baseball fan stalking his favourite player (Wesley Snipes). *The Fan* marked the first time that De Niro seemed to be on autopilot, and the character he portrays seems a veritable caricature of previous De Niro creations.

This film is easily one of the worst baseball-themed movies of all time. Adapted for the screen by Phoef Sutton from the novel by popular crime writer Peter Abrahams, the script is full of glaring errors and improbabilities: a left-handed catcher (well it's not, strictly speaking, impossible, but in one hundred and fifty years of pro baseball, there has only been one); agents who have unlimited access to the clubhouse and follow their clients around everywhere (let's see you try this, Scott Boras!); batters who walk directly from the dugout to the plate without waiting their turn in the on-deck circle—at one point a player walks right past his teammate standing in the on-deck circle. And on, and on.

If you want to see two very good baseball movies that are rather obscure but still available, try *Soul of the Game* (1996, HBO) and *61* (2001, HBO). The first explores, with sensitivity and intelligence, the struggles of Black players trying to make it to the majors in the late forties; the latter paints an engaging portrait of Roger Maris as he struggled with the ghost of Babe Ruth in 1961. Both feature strong scripts, excellent performances—Barry Pepper is outstanding as Maris—and more importantly, they get their baseball right.

Fantastic Voyage

Classic Film
Review

(1966)

When I was eight years old, I had never given much thought to the idea that there was a whole world inside the human body. That world was revealed in one of the most entertaining and imaginative science-fiction movies ever produced: *Fantastic Voyage* (dir. Richard Fleischer). I saw it on the big screen when it was first released, and I will forever be grateful to my older sister, Ginette, for taking me to see this mindblower.

Turning the camera inward for a trip through the human body, *Fantastic Voyage* presents an engaging premise: both the Soviets and the Americans have developed a technology that allows men and machines to be miniaturized, but the technique is profoundly flawed. Anyone or anything miniaturized begins to expand back to normal size after sixty minutes. A scientist from the Eastern Bloc has solved the time-limitation hurdle and is willing to defect to the West, but before he can share his knowledge, his car is attacked by enemy agents and he suffers a life-threatening brain injury. Hoping to save his life, a top-secret government organization assembles a five-person crew led by Stephen Boyd and Arthur Kennedy—including Donald Pleasence, who turns out to be (surprise, surprise) a saboteur. The mission is simple (!): they will board a submarine, the *Proteus*, which will then be miniaturized and injected into the scientist-defector. The crew—also including Raquel Welch as a medical assistant—will then have sixty minutes to make its way through the bloodstream to the man's brain. Using a laser weapon, they will then dissolve the potentially fatal blood clot. Time is of the essence because after exactly sixty minutes they will begin expanding back to their normal size, and things will get extremely messy as the body's immune system begins to attack and destroy the intruders.

Fantastic Voyage—the first sci-fi film I ever saw on the big screen—is an eye-popping feast of spectacular special effects. I vividly remember sitting in wide-eyed amazement as giant globules and corpuscles and blood cells floated magically around the submarine, while arteries became huge tunnels and ventricles opened and closed like gigantic bellows and curtains. I was so astonished that I didn't even ask for popcorn.

And even though I was only eight at the time, I was also astonished by Raquel Welch.

Ms. Welch certainly received far more attention for the fur bikini she wore in *One Million Years B.C.* (1966, dir. Don Chaffey [UK]; released February 1967 in the US), but the white, skin-tight wetsuit she wore in *Fantastic Voyage* at least deserves honourable mention.

Unfortunately, the underwater scenes of the crew swimming outside the sub were actually shot on a sound stage. I say unfortunately because even though I didn't know this when I first saw the film, it seemed to me that there was something unusual about the way the actors moved while swimming. I had seen quite a lot of underwater footage by that time (*Voyage to the Bottom of the Sea* was extremely popular on television), and something just didn't look right. I later learned that the actors were not immersed in water at all but rather suspended from wires. Their movements were photographed at a faster speed, and then played back at normal speed to give the illusion of water resistance. It was all very well done, but wires are wires, and there are a few scenes where the subterfuge shows. Suspend your disbelief accordingly.

The memorable—and not at all exploitative—scene of the male crew members removing clinging antibodies from Ms. Welch's wetsuit presented its own unique challenges. The first time this scene was attempted, the male crew members were extremely careful not to place their hands anywhere near her breasts.

This gave the scene an artificial, strangely comical look, and so the scene was attempted again. The second time around, the actors all reached for her chest. This didn't really work either, for obvious reasons. Eventually, the director told each actor exactly where he should place his hands, and the scene achieved the necessary verisimilitude without being slapped with an R rating.

For several days after I saw *Fantastic Voyage*, I couldn't stop thinking and talking about it. Movies have astonished me many times since, but I have never been so effectively transported into another world as I was on that Saturday afternoon in 1966. In 2008 a newly digitally restored DVD of the film was released. If you haven't seen this in years (or ever), it is well worth your time. The story remains an engaging adventure/thriller and the special effects are superb, even by today's ultra-slick, computer-generated standards.

The special-effects team was under the supervision of the legendary L.B. Abbott (1908–1985), who had supervised the special effects for *The Day the Earth Stood Still* and would go on to work on *Planet of the Apes* and *The Poseidon Adventure.* His resourcefulness in creating those pre-computer visual effects is astonishing. The famous whirlpool scene, which occurs soon after the miniaturized sub has been injected into the body, was created by filling a large punch bowl with a mix of milk and strawberry juice (to simulate the colour of blood at the microscopic level) to which was added three cups of Cheerios. A two-inch miniature model of the sub was then dropped into the bowl, and the mixture was filmed while it was being energetically swirled around. The result is quite convincing. The bonus DVD included in the 2008 release reveals many of the secrets behind the marvellous special effects. *Fantastic Voyage* is a jewel of sci-fi filmmaking.

Funkytown

(2011)

Warning: the following film review contains references to drugs and numerous negative comments about disco music. I apologize in advance to anyone who may have fond memories of the disco era.

Funkytown stars Patrick Huard, who is a hugely popular star in Québec. He is a kind of renaissance entertainer; he began as a stand-up comic, and he has done television and films, both drama and comedy. He starred in the film *Bon Cop, Bad Cop*, which was a big box-office hit in *La Belle Province* even though it suffered from a wildly uneven script. But *Funkytown* may well prove to be his finest hour, or rather two hours. *Funkytown* is directed by Daniel Roby and written by Steve Galluccio (who previously wrote the screenplay for *Mambo Italiano*, a film about a young man from an Italian family in Montréal who decides to come out of the closet). Galluccio was born in Montréal, and his script for *Funkytown* perfectly evokes the particularities of the disco era as it unfurled in that city (in both official languages) while acknowledging a certain debt to both *Saturday Night Fever* and *Boogie Nights*.

I don't know if disco music really had a peak, but *Saturday Night Fever* came out in 1977 and at that point it seemed like most of the culture hopped on the bandwagon. Some keen observers of social trends have said that by the time a new phenomenon is embraced by the middle class and the middle aged, it is effectively dead. I remember in 1970 when my father started wearing three-piece suits with bellbottom pants; by 1979 there were a lot of middle-aged accountants and insurance agents dressing up like John Travolta and snorting copious amounts of coke and/or Johnson's baby powder. And I vaguely recall that girls became very skinny — they were probably snorting Diet Coke.

I absolutely hated everything about disco: the ridiculous clothes, the monotonous music, the monotonous attitude (i.e., self-identifying by dressing and acting and behaving like everyone else), and the ridiculous drugs. Someone said once that cocaine made him feel like a new man, but the problem was that the first thing the new man wanted was more cocaine. I thought disco was a kind of fascist pop music born of an increasingly stifling corporate culture. It had that incessant, repetitive, thudding, hammer-to-the-head mindless beat that seemed perfect for marching around in jackboots. The low point came with the release of that horrific album of Beatles' tunes remixed to a disco beat. In 1979 I cheered as a Disco Demolition Night was held at Comiskey Park in Chicago.

But disco was big money and the second most famous disco in North America, after Studio 54 in New York, was The Lime Light in Montréal. In *Funkytown*, the disco is called The Starlight, and for much of the film a rumour circulates that Mick Jagger is going to drop in. It seems that Bowie himself has told Mick that The Starlight is the hippest place in town.

Huard portrays Bastien Lavallée, a hotshot radio personality who hosts a popular disco dance party on local television as well as being the DJ at the Starlight disco. The film follows Bastien's coke-fuelled vertiginous career spiral to the top and, inevitably, back down to the bottom. The character is based on real-life radio/TV host Alain Montpetit, who was the high-flying "king of disco radio" in Montréal in the late seventies and early eighties. Montpetit was found dead of a cocaine overdose in a hotel room in 1987. Fifteen years later, New York police pinned an unsolved murder on him. Police discovered that five years before his overdose, he had murdered a top French-Canadian model named Marie-Josée St-Antoine, stabbing her to death in her New York apartment. Even though these elements are explored, *Funkytown* is not a murder mystery or a cop movie; it is an engaging, fast-paced ride that follows seven characters though the golden days of disco in Montréal.

The cast is composed of Canadian and American actors, and it is very strong. The film is in both English and French with English predominating. The pop-culture sensibilities of the era—highlighting the prevailing American culture—and the desire of the Québécois characters to be cool, to speak English, to be hip and American is perfectly captured in the script's Franglais dialogues. Huard's character, a francophone married to an anglophone, has an anglophone top-model mistress who he is trying to turn into a TV personality despite the girl's complete ineptitude in front of a camera. His speech switches constantly between French and English, sometimes in the same sentence—a pattern repeated by many of the characters in the film. Well-known Québec actor Paul Doucet portrays the super-flamboyant Jonathan Aaronson, who is based on another real-life media personality of the time, a fashion, gossip, and trends columnist named Douglas (Coco) Leopold who was ubiquitous in the disco era. I remember him doing his What's In and What's Out column on French-language television where he would give his viewers the up-to-the-minute lowdown of what was hot and what was not. Coco, a flamboyant gay man, was quite entertaining to watch. Doucet could easily have turned him into a caricature—in real life, Coco was cartoonish—but Doucet toned him down a bit and made him rather endearing, and totally believable.

Ensemble pieces can quickly become messy, but this script stays focused, doing a good job of navigating the often intertwined subplots. The look of the film is museum perfect, complete with shots of the Olympic Stadium and René Lévesque on television. Québec in 1976 was of course an exciting, tumultuous time—the Montréal Olympics occupied the world stage that summer, and then the Parti Québécois came to power in November; while many believed that Québec was on the verge of nationhood, the regulars of the Starlight disco in *Funkytown* feel at best annoyed or at worst threatened by the surge in Québec nationalism. As one character says bluntly, "here we are partying and making a fortune in the modern world, and these idiots want to bring us back to birch-bark canoes!" The script could have focused solely on Huard's character—there is enough there—but the numerous subplots do offer the viewer some interesting side trips, for instance, when a young couple who dream of stardom get their big chance dancing at the Starlight. They are called Tina and Tino, they are engaged, and Tino's widowed mother, who runs the family's Italian restaurant, is extremely hostile toward her son's dreams of dancing fame — echoing the dramatic situation in *Saturday Night Fever*. Tino, conflicted between helping his mother run the restaurant and being a dancer, is also conflicted sexually and is ripe for the picking as the flamboyant fashion columnist Jonathan sets his sights on him.

Funkytown is one of the best Québec productions of the last decade. Its main weakness lies in its overly ambitious script that is subplot heavy to say the least — there is enough material here for a six-hour miniseries. And by trying to neatly tie up all of the dramatic threads at the end, the film winds up with a bloated running time of 132 minutes. That being said, the movie is saved by the strong cast, a superb performance by Patrick Huard, and great atmosphere. Connoisseurs of the disco era will note certain historical inaccuracies (e.g., release dates for certain songs) but *Funkytown* gets it right when it comes to the most important element: capturing the spirit and mood of a specific time and place.

Gone

(20/2)

What in heck ever happened to the art of the movie trailer? Trailers used to tease and intrigue and promise; now they go on and on and give away the whole movie. When I saw the trailer for *Gone*, I thought, not another one of these movies where this very attractive young woman named Jill claims to have been kidnapped by a serial killer, and then managed to escape from a deep hole in the forest where she was being kept; but the cops never believed her and she wound up in a psychiatric hospital for a while until she went to live with her equally attractive sister, Molly, who appears now to have been kidnapped by the same man but the cops still don't believe it; and she probably has less than a day to find her sister with the cops hot on her trail because they think she is a dangerous nut . . . not another one of these!

Gone is directed by Heitor Dhalia, who is Brazilian. I was not familiar with his previous work but I have to say that he does have style. He also has one silly, lame-brained script to deal with. This is a good-looking movie, however, and it does have some well-orchestrated chase scenes and a few crumbs of engaging suspense.

Amanda Seyfried portrays the attractive green-eyed blonde who is either suffering from post-traumatic stress disorder (her story) or is just spectacularly cuckoo (the cops' opinion). As one leering detective tells another, "can I take her home? I like them a little crazy." The script does not overly tax Ms. Seyfried's acting chops; mostly she gets to run around (a lot), and walk around (at night), and drive (like a lunatic), all the while looking either gravely worried or totally freaked out. She also yells a lot, mostly at the cops. I don't know what kind of pills she kept popping (I suppose they are tranquilizers), but for all the effect they have on her behaviour they might as well be Smarties. The music does its best to add some atmosphere—it shouts and blares and underlines and emphasizes in that not-too-subtle, creepy-movie-music way—but in the end, it's *peine perdue*.

Ms. Seyfried does not lack screen charisma—she recently made the Annual Independent Critics List of the 100 Most Beautiful Famous Faces from around the World—but she has that petite-blonde look that makes her appear to be a genetically engineered product of the All-American Sports Star Trophy Wife Company of Antioch, Illinois. I'm sorry, but these blonde starlets all look the same to me. Her older sister, Molly, portrayed by Emily Wickersham, has a more mature and interesting look. I would have been curious to see how this would have turned out if the two had switched roles and Jill had been the kidnappee. As it stands, Molly gets to spend most of the movie off screen—she is gone after all—and when we do see her she is writhing around with duct tape over her mouth. This made it darn near impossible for me to determine if she had any acting chops, although the writhing seemed convincing.

Gone is written by Allison Burnett, and I am afraid that his script is in such a terrific hurry to get things going that it makes some very poor choices. Very early on, in a brief flashback, we see that our heroine Jill has been abducted sometime in the past. If this crucial plot element had been revealed gradually, only after the sister Molly disappeared, it would have been much more effective. But the script is like a five-year-old nephew who can't keep a secret; it wants to tell us everything at once. Of course there isn't really anything new under the sun when it comes to movies about kidnapped girls being held in wells by serial killers, but the script constructs a veritable skyscraper-sized pile of clichés.

It wasn't that long ago that cell phones were such a novelty that entire movies were built around them. Remember *Cellular*? In that one, all the phone could do was make and receive phone calls—how boring is that?—but it was enough to fuel a script back in 2004. Now cell phones in movies are omnipresent and are often used as pivotal plot devices. In *Gone*, there is a whole lot of cell phone talkin' goin' on. But the crucial scene where the heroine is being directed by the supposed killer to the place where she believes her sister is being held—far out in the woods in a national park—should be enshrined in the Cell Phone Silliness Hall of Fame. The scene features a cell phone that couldn't possibly work under those particular circumstances but does; like the cell phones in the television series *24* that work despite being in a high-security, armour-plated, electronically shielded bunker, or the cell phones in the Chris O'Donnell thriller *Vertical Limit* that work at 20,000 feet—although only when one of the characters has to reveal some deep dark secret to another character. In *Gone*, the cell phone starts to lose its signal as the heroine gets deeper and deeper into the forest. Then the killer on the line says, "goodbye; there is no service here." Uno momento, por favor.

The killer is even deeper into the forest than our heroine, so explain to me, Edison, how his phone could be working? Is our heroine perhaps the victim of a mysterious robocall like those which misdirected voters during the Canadian Federal Election of 2011?

Let's talk about characters in movies whose sole purpose is to rouse our suspicions. *Gone* is set in Portland, Oregon—a picturesque place that seems in this movie to be populated almost exclusively by people who might as well have PROBABLE SUSPECT tattooed on their foreheads. We get a very creepy looking detective (Wes Bentley), a father and son team of locksmiths who would not be out of place playing banjos in *Deliverance*, a squirrely janitor who looks like he must also own either a banjo or a chainsaw (or both), plus an assortment of characters who all behave so suspiciously that I immediately knew that none of them were even remotely involved in the crime.

Gone contains quite a bit of unintentionally funny dialogue, as in this exchange:

Jill: My sister has disappeared!
Detective Bozeman: Mrs. Conway! Adults have the right to disappear.

Despite scintillating dialogue like this, nothing can replace verisimilitude in a thriller—a vital ingredient that has, alas, apparently gone missing along with the sister.

As another car chase unfolded onscreen, I started to wonder why Jill was wasting her time as a waitress when she could be working as a highly paid stunt driver. The way she bombs around Portland in her Volkswagen Golf is death defying. I hadn't seen this kind of wild abandon behind the wheel since Michael Schumacher bounced off the guard rails at the 1994 Australian Grand Prix. Unfortunately, there's no way to drive around the bottomless plot holes that litter the script. That being said, *Gone* could be a fun rental. You could invite the gang over, split up into teams, and play spot-the-suspect or spot-the-plot-hole. Give yourself bonus points if you find it extremely hard to swallow that a young woman who has been kidnapped and brutally held against her will, and whose tormentor was never caught, would be—just one year later—working the night shift at an all-night diner and parking far enough away from the diner that she has to walk, alone, to and from her car. How do you say "give me a break" in Spanish?

Grindhouse

Shoot, Slash, and Splat

(2007)

Having two filmmakers, Quentin Tarantino and Robert Rodriguez, work together to present a double feature for the price of one admission sounds like a great idea. I'm certainly all for giving the movie public more bang for its buck. By all means bring back double features, and by all means bring back the cartoons that we used to get before the main attraction. Unfortunately, the double bill that *Grindhouse* offers us is a celebration of the trash-and-slash exploitation films of the seventies. Did we really need to bring those back? And what the heck is a grind house anyway?

I know what a grinder is. A grinder is a baseball game whose pace slows to a crawl and neither team seems capable of winning.

According to Monsieur Tarantino, a grind house was one of those sleazy movie theatres that used to show exploitation films back in the seventies and eighties. They were dark, dingy theatres that projected scratchy prints, sometimes with missing reels; the antithesis of today's vast, colourful, antiseptic Cineplexes with their digital projectors. Why anyone would be nostalgic for these dumps and for the films they used to show — films with titles like *Biker Chicks from Zombietown* or *Children Shouldn't Play with Dead Things* — is a bit of a mystery to me, although I do understand the perverse attraction that trash culture exerts on some people. And from his very first film, *Reservoir Dogs*, Tarantino's guiding principle seems to be that not only can trash be art, but if something is trashy enough, it automatically becomes art.

90

This is not a principle I agree with (and this is an understatement). Let's also be certain that we don't confuse low budget with low quality. Because a film is made on a shoestring doesn't automatically make it trash. Trash is a matter of sensibility (or lack of it), not dollars and cents. And I have always said that many low-budget B movies are wonderfully entertaining. What makes a film entertaining is the quality of the story: the quality of the ideas being explored and the quality of the director and actors involved in the exploration. But in *Grindhouse* we're not talking about B movies, we're talking about Z movies, la crème de la crap of exploitation films. Listeners who have been tuning into my reviews for years know that I do not like Quentin Tarantino's movies; his are movies that celebrate junk culture as if it was high art and pander to the lowest cultural denominators while glorifying brutality.

Part one of this double bill is *Planet Terror* by Robert Rodriguez, who previously directed *Once Upon a Time in Mexico*, which I found profoundly silly and brutally violent. Here's a quote that a moviegoer who had just seen *Planet Terror* posted on the Internet (I assume that the comment comes from a male audience member because the audience for this kind of schlock is almost exclusively male): "there is so much blood and gore in this movie that it has never become so enjoyable to see someone getting shot before."

I couldn't have said it better myself.

Rather than give a full-scale plot synopsis of *Planet Terror*, allow me instead to simply mention some highlights: an experimental nerve gas is released in Texas—where else?—and this gas turns people into flesh-eating zombies. Original, *non*?

This gas also makes the victim's skin bubble and ooze, and decompose and turn into goo resembling half-congealed raspberry Jell-O. Our heroine is a one-legged, ex-go-go dancer named Cherry. Her mechanic boyfriend replaces her prosthetic leg with a machine gun (!), which she then uses to splatter the zombies and anyone else who gets in her way. Along the way we are treated to the usual scenes of exploding heads, eyes poked out with various sharp objects, bodies ripped in half, and a veritable festival of decapitation and castration. *Planet Terror* makes *Texas Chainsaw Massacre* look like *Mary Poppins.*

Before all of you Rodriguez/Tarantino fans slam this book down in disgust while muttering "he doesn't *get* it! It's satire!" allow me to say that I fully understand that the script (such as it is) has its tongue firmly in its cheek. The problem is that the tongue is black and lumpy and keeps falling onto the blood-splattered floor.

Granted, some of the violence is so ridiculously excessive that even I had to laugh—in one postmodern moment the blood actually splatters onto the camera lens. But most of the violence is neither satirical nor postmodern; it is just gratuitous and disgusting. I object to movies that present themselves as being superior to what they are satirizing just because they are intentionally rotten. Whether or not your movie is intentionally or unintentionally rotten, guess what? It is *still* rotten. Satire is not automatically achieved because a filmmaker reproduces, to the extreme, all of the elements that made something deserving of receiving a satirical treatment in the first place. If your so-called satire merely recreates—indeed, jazzes up and positively glorifies—all of the cheesy, sleazy elements of exploitation films, where exactly is the satire and what have you accomplished? If you want to see a real parody of zombie films—a shining example of what satire is supposed to be when it doesn't totally confuse itself with the subject it purports to be satirizing—check out *Fido*, a Canadian film that is discussed earlier on in my review of *28 Weeks Later*. That one is worth seeing.

After *Planet Terror*, we have an old-style intermission of sorts that consists of three or four trailers for fictitious films. These are followed by Tarantino's film *Death Proof*. The whole *Grindhouse* experience has a running time of approximately three hours (two ninety-minute movies plus ten or fifteen minutes of trailers). Actually, the phony trailers are much better than the features. We get trailers for movies with titles like *Werewolf Women of the SS* and a horror film trailer called *Don't!*, a parody of horror movies like *Don't Look in the Basement*. Another is for a movie called *Hobo with a Shotgun*, which I think needs no further explanation.

In the Tarantino entry, *Death Proof*, Kurt Russell portrays a serial killer who uses his car to kill women. Near the end, the tables are turned by a group of women led by real-life stuntwoman Zoe Bell, and they give old Kurt the boot, literally. After catching him in an exciting car chase, they beat him to death with boots and a metal pipe. In Tarantino's universe, this is a feel-good moment.

Tarantino is much more than an idiot with a camera. It would be so much easier to dismiss this nonsense if he was an incompetent director, but he has enough talent to be taken seriously. The car chases here are excellent. But a car chase does not a movie make. And the rest of it is either boring or silly or just plain brutal. I don't want to sound like Dr. Phil and start analyzing the brutality and misogyny that run deep in Tarantino's movies, but I will say that movies like *Death Proof* raise the issue of why there is so much violence against women in movies, and why so many men think that violence is both sexy and entertaining.

Defenders of Tarantino—and he doesn't really need any as this is criticism, not an attack—have said that his later films like *Kill Bill* and *Kill Bill Vol. 2* along with this latest *Death Proof* are empowering to women. To me, this seems off the mark by a mile. To empower females, I believe that a director has to do more than give the girls some guns and have them behave as brutally and insanely as the guys. How are you projecting a positive, empowering image of women if they are running around in sexy clothes killing everything that moves? In what way does it empower women to depict them indulging in endless revenge, castration, and decapitation fantasies while wearing tight leather, prosthetic machine guns, and lingerie?

I also take issue with the idea that if you don't like Tarantino you aren't hip. Surely there is more to being hip than wallowing in violent, juvenile pseudo-porn.

At the end of *Grindhouse*, I suddenly realized the true meaning of the title: I felt like my brain had been put through a coffee grinder. That being said, if you decide to sit through this and you find it funny and entertaining, well, who am I to tell you that you're wrong? I'm a critic, Jim, not a TV psychologist!

The Happening

(2008)

In 1936, Eddie Morgan was a twenty-one-year-old rookie with the St. Louis Cardinals. He hit a home run on his very first at-bat in the majors. In fact, he hit a home run on the very first pitch he ever saw in the majors. And it was the only home run he ever hit.

M. Night Shyamalan is the Eddie Morgan of film directors. He hit a towering home run with his first film, *The Sixth Sense*, in 1999, but then he started striking out and struggling: *Unbreakable*, *Signs*, *The Village*, *Lady in the Water*, and now *The Happening*. I see a dead career.

On the plus side, his movies are stylish, and he knows how to create tension by keeping the frame tight and not showing us too much so that we always have the feeling that something terrible is lurking just outside the frame. Unfortunately, what is lurking just outside the frame is rarely terrible, and often just terribly silly.

The music heard in Shyamalan's films is usually effective if somewhat bombastic, often used for shock effect. His composer of choice is James Newton Howard. Howard composed a brilliant score for *Batman Begins* (2005); it was both minimalistic and punchy. I have often said that when it comes to film scores, less is more. Shyamalan seems to bring out the more in Howard rather than the less. His score for *The Happening* is overwrought.

The ability to create tension in a scene doesn't necessarily translate into the ability to generate real, sustained suspense for the duration of a film. Shyamalan has style, but that has never been a substitute for substance. His movies usually start well, piquing our interest with an intriguing premise, but then his scripts often wander off and lose themselves in the woods. His stories tend to unravel and lose focus, which is the kiss of death if your number one objective is to keep the audience in a state of fear.

The Happening begins on a summer morning in Central Park in New York. People are strolling, chatting, and walking their dogs. Two young women are sitting on a bench. Suddenly everyone stops; some people begin to walk backwards and screams are heard. A cop who had been chatting with a cabbie pulls out his service revolver and shoots himself; the cabbie steps out of his cab, picks up the revolver, and does the same. People start committing suicide everywhere in the park. It's a great start — in terms of a scary movie, I mean, not in terms of a summer morning. The shock value is enormous; it grabs our attention. Cut to a high school science class in Philadelphia. Elliot (Mark Wahlberg) is teaching a class, and the subject is why honey bees are disappearing from many parts of the United States. Shyamalan's script introduces an intriguing element borrowed from real life: honey bee populations have indeed declined in the past couple of years, and this has some scientists very concerned. But what does this have to do with the plot?

Good question. The movie appears to be setting itself up as an ecological-disaster story. The script even throws in a quote often attributed to Einstein, that "the decline of honey bees will signal the end for mankind" — although *The New Quotable Einstein* states that Einstein probably never said this. Bee populations started to decline fifty years after he died, and anyway, Einstein was a physicist, not an entomologist.

Our hero soon learns that there has been some kind of attack on New York City, possibly a terrorist attack. Are these mass suicides the result of some kind of chemical weapon, a new kind of nerve gas? Elliot and his best friend, Julian (John Leguizamo), decide to head out of the city accompanied by Julian's eight-year-old daughter, Jess, and wife, Alma (Zooey Deschanel). From this point on the script, like the fabric of society, begins to rapidly unravel.

As in most of his previous films, Shyamalan simply refuses to let the story evolve at its own pace, precipitating the dramatic events much too rapidly. He immediately reveals the cause of the crisis — poof! there goes the mystery — and he introduces a subplot that places Elliot's marriage in jeopardy by suggesting that Alma is having an affair.

My eyes started to roll back in my head. Who cares about Elliot's marriage!

The world is coming to an end and people are committing mass suicide. It should be enough that a major city is under some form of mysterious attack and that the characters have decided to flee to the countryside. I understand that Shyamalan is injecting this element into the plot in order to flesh out Elliot's character, but he is really just making the already murky dramatic waters even muddier. Another unfortunate side effect of this revelation is that it makes Alma's character less sympathetic to the audience; not a good idea if you have a dwindling group of survivors placed in peril. The audience needs to care deeply about what happens to all of the main characters, not be given the opportunity to respond with, "oh, she deserved it, she was cheating on the hero!"

Pretty soon our little group has boarded a train, and panic is in the air as reports start coming in from people with cell phones and BlackBerrys that the attacks are spreading across New England and the Eastern seaboard. With all of this rapidly increasing chaos, I was skeptical that cell phones and BlackBerrys would still be working, but c'est possible, I suppose. But then our brave little group is stranded in a small town when the train stops because the engineers have lost all contact with the outside world.

Zooey Deschanel portrays Mark Wahlberg's wife. She played Trillian in The Hitchhiker's Guide to the Galaxy, and she provided the voice of Lani in Surf's Up. Her big blue eyes fill the screen and she exudes charisma. Unfortunately, in this movie she behaves as if the director has forced her to inhale some of the toxin that's making everyone crazy—her performance is reminiscent of Screwball Squirrel. Indeed, most of the cast seems to have deeply inhaled some kind of weird, airborne, toxic substance that has temporarily muddled their acting skills. Wahlberg in particular gives an uncharacteristically self-conscious performance. Throughout the film he seems to be searching desperately for his motivation. The dialogue that Shyamalan has written for him doesn't help one bit.

Elliot: You know that everyone gives off energy, right? It's scientifically proven. They got these cameras that can record what color you are when you're feeling different things. People that are angry give off a different color than people that are sad. See this ring? This ring can supposedly tell you what you're feeling. Let's see what you're feeling right now.

The hero of the movie is a science teacher and he's talking about mood rings? No wonder the world is doomed.

Shyamalan's script is a cringe-inducing vehicle for stilted, silly dialogue, the kind of dialogue that emerges when a screenwriter is desperately trying to give his characters depth or scrambling to explain a murky plot point to the audience. In *The Happening*, characters are constantly telling each other things that they obviously should know and could not possibly have forgotten. An especially bad moment occurs near the very end when we are treated to what I call the "couple about to die and reminiscing about things that obviously never happened" scene. I felt embarrassed for everyone involved.

Many in the supporting cast of characters seem to have walked directly out of a Warner Bros. cartoon. Loony characters have always been staples of end-of-the-world movies, but the looniness is much more effective when it is a gradual process.

I haven't even mentioned plot holes. Here's a doozy: the toxin is airborne, yet whenever a character wants to remain safe, he or she closes the windows and doors. I'll bet you weren't aware that air doesn't penetrate the house when the doors and windows are closed. So why are the heating bills so high? Also, if the toxin is airborne, why does it not go beyond the borders of the East Coast of the United States? Wind doesn't stop at borders—although in Ottawa, most of the hot air does seem to settle over Parliament Hill.

I'll be blunt: I will never again review a film directed by Shyamalan unless he gets someone else to write the screenplay. I have had my fill. And it's too bad because he has some good ideas but his stories don't deliver the goods. If you're in the mood for a first-rate end-of-the world movie, try *On the Beach* with Ava Gardner and Gregory Peck, or *The Birds*, or *The Day the Earth Caught Fire.*

The Happening is not happening, man.

The Hobbit: An Unexpected Journey

(2012)

Here I go with a review of the most hyped movie of recent memory: the first film in the *Hobbit* trilogy, from the hand of director Peter Jackson who gave us the *Lord of the Rings* trilogy some ten years ago.

Wait a minute. Hobbit trilogy?

Two questions inevitably come to mind: how and why? How can Tolkien's charming three-hundred-page book possibly be turned into three two-and-a-half-hour plus movies? Well, it's quite simple. You have to throw in a ton of stuff that isn't in the book—battles, battles, and more battles—and multiple, winding subplots. This is not so much a question of fleshing out *The Hobbit* as it is of bloating and stretching it beyond recognition. As for why this is being done, well, as Rod Serling might have put it: the answer consists of one little five-letter word that makes men's eyes turn into shining pinballs; a word that bounces around in the brain gleefully—clouding all thought as it rings like the clear chime of an overheated cash register on a busy Saturday afternoon at Macy's. The word is "greed."

I remember reading *The Hobbit* many years ago at a single sitting—one of the few books I've ever read at one sitting. I loved it. It was sweet and funny and poetic. I thought it far superior to *The Lord of the Rings* because it was a gentle miniature, and I don't just mean the hero. I mean that it wasn't overblown with sweeping, bloody battles and pompous poems and huge, Middle-Earth-shaking themes—although there was quite a lot riding on little Bilbo's shoulders. But I read the book as an allegory about the passage from childhood to adulthood. When it was originally published in 1937, it was considered children's literature and was reviewed (extremely positively) accordingly. It is a wonderful, fanciful tale about growing up—Bilbo grows as a person (as a hobbit anyway) and discovers the meaning of friendship and responsibility. He also learns firsthand of the wonders and the terrors that await us all in that big world that surrounds our safe and comfortable little homes. And I certainly found it easy to identify with the reluctant hero—there is more Bilbo than Gandalf in all of us. Unfortunately, this film adaptation strays, and strays, and stretchessss it does, Preciousssss, stretchesss, the story Preciousss . . . to fill time it does . . . nasssty script.

Let's talk about the science of filmmaking. The path that Peter Jackson has chosen is a technologically innovative and controversial one.

For ninety years, the cinema standard has been to shoot at 24 frames per second (fps). As we know, movement in cinema is an illusion—what we are actually seeing is twenty-four single photographs passing by our eyes every second. The standard for HD TV is 30 fps. The human eye is capable of seeing much faster, about 100 fps, but we long ago settled on 24 fps because it represented the best compromise between what looks right and what is economically viable. In the many decades when actual film stock was being used, we can well imagine the enormous costs that would have been incurred if the frame rate was faster—faster rate equals more film consumed. Wishing to take advantage of the very latest technology, Peter Jackson decided to shoot *The Hobbit* at a high frame rate of 48 fps, twice the industry standard. The results are mixed to say the least.

On the one hand we are presented with a crystal-clear image, without any of the blurring that naturally accompanies movement in a standard film. Of course, this slight blurring is no big deal; it is simply what movies look like, or at least it was until now. But watching *The Hobbit* at 48 fps was a highly disconcerting experience—my son compared it to being on set and watching the actors performing while looking through a window. For me it felt like I was seeing a very elaborate, staged HD television program. Everything—the sets, the props—looked somehow fake. And because there is not the slightest blurring, the actors looked vaguely unreal, a bit like Play-Doh. They seemed to move too fast, which made their performances strangely artificial. And the (too numerous) battle scenes looked as sharp and flat as Sunday Night Football in HD.

I'm sorry if all of this sounds like I'm having one of those legendary acid flashbacks we've all heard too much about—plasticine hobbits with looking-glass ties—but the entire visual experience was bizarre, and definitely unsatisfying. After about twenty minutes I wasn't so distracted, but I never really got used to it, and I'm sure I never will.

Peter Jackson has been quick to defend his choice, pointing out that "young people like it." Well, teenagers haven't been conditioned by watching movies for forty years so they are open to something different, but is different synonymous with better? The human brain can get used to just about anything—remember orange shag carpet—but what does that prove? When CDs first appeared and older recordings were transferred onto CD, they sounded terrible because the digital technology boosted the high end, making the music sound harsh and thin. But the music industry kept saying, "you'll get used to it; this is better, this is clearer." But guess what? A few years later (after they'd ripped us off for millions with these crummy CDs) they realized that they had to remaster all of the older analog recordings in order to make music sound natural, as it was recorded. Now kids are used to the mp3 standard, which is terribly compressed—losing a whole spectrum of sound colour—but they have grown up with it and don't know what they're missing. I think that the 48 fps rate is an analogous phenomenon. It may well catch on with young or even older filmgoers, and become a standard, but I seriously doubt it. Call me Barney Rubble (go ahead!) but some things don't need to be digitized, sanitized, polarized, and transmogrified—they're just fine the way they are.

The Hobbit probably doesn't need a plot synopsis, but brief-ly: A hobbit named Bilbo Baggins is recruited, extremely reluc-tantly, by the wizard Gandalf the Grey to go on an adventure. The objective is to help a company of thirteen dwarves—led by Thorin Oakenshield—win back their kingdom under the moun-tain, which is presently occupied by the terrifying dragon Smaug. During the adventure, while he is lost in a dark cave deep under-ground, Bilbo meets with a strange and pathetic creature named Gollum. They engage in a game of riddles that Bilbo must win to gain his freedom. Gollum drops a magical ring (his Preciousss) and Bilbo steals it from the wretched creature. The ring allows him to become invisible, but it also possesses a terrible power that becomes an overwhelming burden, slowly amplifying the ring bearer's darker side. The story is populated by encounters with all kinds of wondrous and terrible creatures: evil orcs, terrible gob-lins, and the beautiful elves of Rivendell.

Ah, Rivendell—not to be confused with Riverdale. The for-mer has elves; the latter has Archie and Jughead and the gang, and who knows? Archie may show up in the second instalment—dras-tic measures have to be taken to stretch this little book into three epic movies. I could see Veronica as an evil, yet fetching, sorceress with Reggie as her no-good acolyte.

— — —

The Hobbit presents us with some stunningly beautiful land-scapes, wondrous castles, and magical, impossible cities—Riven-dell is particularly beautiful. There are also some amazing, terrible creatures like orcs that will cause Tolkien fans to rejoice. Mar-tin Freeman (*The Hitchhiker's Guide to the Galaxy*) is excellent as Bilbo, and Cate Blanchett as the Elf Queen Galadriel is every hobbit's dream. Andy Serkis via motion-capture reprises his role as Gollum, and he is suitably over the top—manic and mania-cal, frantic and tragic. But what have they done to his voice? I strained to understand every other word. This Gollum sounds like Daffy Duck on helium, which is a major disappointment because the encounter with Gollum and the subsequent game of riddles is a highlight of the book, and it is pretty much unintelligible here.

The full title of Jackson's film is *The Hobbit: An Unexpected Journey*, but it could have been called *The Hobbit: A Carefully Calculated Cash Grab*. There is just too much money to be made. The film contains some moments of magic, but it also has tons of filler and scenes that go on too long. And when it comes to the battles, it seems like the script has taken a page from *Monty Python and the Holy Grail* with Gandalf shouting every fifteen minutes to "Run, Run!" There are battles with orcs, with goblins, with trolls, and with orcs again.

Exciting? Not really.

The Hobbit plays out like the action-packed, video-game battle version of the book. And in a flashback scene we get a glimpse of the dragon Smaug attacking a city, but of course we don't really see it because this is being saved for part two. We can look forward to a lot of hype in 2013 as the dragon's appearance is slowly revealed in an ever annoying series of teasers and trailers.

I hate to rain on the Shire—and this is filmmaking on a monumental scale—but *The Hobbit* does not capture the spirit of the book. It is, if anything, too monumental. It is much closer in spirit to the mood and scale of *The Lord of the Rings.* A shame it is, Preciousss . . . poor little Baggins . . . lost in this huge movie. Lost forever, Preciousss . . .

I Am Legend

(2007)

Richard Matheson's 1954 novel, *I Am Legend,* has been adapted for the big screen three times. The first screen adaptation was an American-Italian coproduction called *L'ultimo uomo della Terra* (The Last Man on Earth). Released in 1964 and directed by Ubaldo Ragona, it starred Vincent Price and an all-Italian cast. Matheson was actually involved in writing the screenplay, which explains why the Vincent Price version is faithful to the novel, but Matheson was so unhappy with the finished product that he had his name changed to Logan Swanson on the screen credits.

The most obvious problem with the film is that Vincent Price is miscast. His stagey theatrical presence—very effective in the numerous gothic-style horror films he made—seems misplaced in a character who is supposed to be a modern-day scientist. But it isn't only Price who looks out of place. The movie was shot in Italy, and as incredible as it may seem, the producers believed (or hoped and prayed) that the outskirts of Rome would pass for New York City. Mamma mia!

— — —

I Am Legend was remade in 1971 as *The Omega Man.* Directed by Boris Sagal, it starred Charlton Heston, an actor who should have been given a special lifetime achievement award by the Academy of Motion Picture Arts and Sciences for jaw-jutting and fist clenching—his two best qualities. Who needs character development when you can jut your jaw so spectacularly? *The Omega Man* was so far removed from the original novel that Matheson was quoted as saying, "it has nothing to do with my book."

This new *I Am Legend* is the third—and hopefully last—attempt at bringing Matheson's story to the big screen. It is directed by Francis Lawrence and stars Will Smith. Francis Lawrence cut his directorial teeth on music videos. For better or ill, music videos have become a training ground for many directors in recent years. While the best of them manage to transcend the limited range of music video, in many cases the audience is assaulted by a feature film that has the attention span of Sarah Palin. The narrative lurches in fits and starts while spitting out images so fast and jumpy that the bewildered viewer has the impression that the film was edited by Daffy Duck on Benzedrine.

You won't be surprised if I tell you that *I Am Legend* has little connection to the original novel. It is a hybrid, which is a more sophisticated way of saying that it is a bit of a mess. It has been quite radically altered to become a commercial Will Smith action flick. The zombies, who are central to the novel, are obviously computer-generated (CGI) and they have been mutated by the screenwriters into video-game super zombies. Perhaps this is the true essence of the virus that has afflicted humanity: it turns everyone into CGI characters.

Youngsters who don't know anything about the original novel but who have been weaned on movies like *28 Days Later* and video games will find themselves on familiar ground. The movie is brutal—sometimes disturbingly so—and frenetic. It also contains enough jump moments to make you spill your popcorn several times. Fans of Matheson's novel will be at best annoyed, at worst bitterly disappointed.

Important note:
> For readers who may not be familiar with the intricate inner workings of the horror-movie industry—and for those of you who didn't read my first book (shame on you!)—allow me to explain that a jump moment is a moment designed specifically to make people jump and spill their popcorn. Later, when the cinema is empty, the staff will go around sweeping up the spilled popcorn so that it can be rebagged and resold. If you think that there are

obscene profits to be made selling ten cents worth of popcorn for four dollars, imagine the fortunes to be generated
by reselling the same popcorn!

Time for the old plot synopsis. It is the near future, and a revo-
lutionary vaccine that cures cancer has been developed. The vaccine is actually a genetically modified strain of the measles. Unfortunately for the human race, after thousands of people have been
vaccinated, it is discovered that the vaccine mutates and transforms humans into raving, bloodthirsty zombies who are acutely
sensitive to sunlight.

Will Smith portrays Robert Neville, a US Army Colonel and
a brilliant scientist who is working to find a cure for the vaccine.
The virus has become airborne and the army has decided to completely quarantine New York City. Although he could escape on
an army helicopter along with his wife and young daughter, our
hero chooses to stay in New York to continue working in his underground laboratory to find a cure. We flash forward three years,
and Neville is now the only living human being in New York
City, but he is not alone. At night he must barricade himself in his
fortress-like house, isolated with his memories and his Bob Mar-
ley CDs, because it is in the dark that the mutated humans come
out searching for blood.

The first twenty-five minutes, when Neville is alone in New
York with his dog and his memories, are by far the best moments
of the film. These early scenes are faithful to the mood of the
original story. The vision of a New York partially covered with
overgrowth — a city empty and decaying — are creepy and highly
effective. The script provides some inspired *mise en scène* as we
see Neville hunting deer in Times Square with his faithful German
Shepherd, Sam. Will Smith carries this first part of the movie very
well, giving a moving portrayal of a dedicated researcher teetering
on the brink of losing his mind to loneliness and discouragement.
Early on there is an exciting action scene as Neville captures a female zombie and takes her back to his lab to test a new vaccine he
has developed. But after these few promising moments, the script
strays very far from the original source material and loses its way.

The script is cowritten by Akiva Goldsman, who is also one of the film's producers. As a screenwriter, Mr. Goldsman has a stunning track record: in 1995 he destroyed *Batman & Robin*, in 1998 he annihilated *Lost in Space*, and in 2004 he adapted (read: mangled) one of the great sci-fi short-story collections of all time, *I, Robot*. His screen adaptation of *Lost in Space* remains particularly notorious; his reckless reworking of the fondly remembered TV show managed to jettison (read: flush down the tubes) everything that had been good about the original series. I have not, nor will I ever, forgive him.

I know what you're thinking; Goldsman's screenplay for *A Beautiful Mind* with Russell Crowe won an Oscar, so he must be talented. But the thing is, even a journeyman baseball player with a lifetime .220 batting average can come into a game and hit a game-winning home run. Writers are like ball players: you have to judge them over a period of time by their averages, not just for that one big hit. Over his career, Akiva Goldsman has been a kind of literary meat grinder, a master at turning strong, even brilliant source material into the cinematic equivalent of Spam—which is what the last survivors of the human race would probably have to live on.

In Matheson's original story, the infected humans mutate gradually and they begin to adapt to their new condition, actually creating a society. They become the new form of humanity that has inherited the earth, and Robert Neville is an anachronism. Worse, the mutants see him as a monster, the last of his kind. He has become legend. Matheson's vision reaches far beyond the action tale to question the very essence of what constitutes humanity. His protagonist is psychologically complex and morally ambiguous.

Enter Akiva Goldsman.

As imagined by him, the zombies are super duper: incredibly strong, agile, and fast, and completely insane and blood-thirsty. They are raving things, so the movie is reduced to its most simplistic terms: hero versus the monsters.

Goldsman's script doesn't even respect its own internal logic. A huge plot hole has the zombies setting a clever trap for our hero, but their previous behaviour has made it glaringly obvious that they do not possess the mental capacity to accomplish this. In the context of what has come before, the scene makes no sense at all—it exists solely to give the canine costar, Sam, an opportunity to behave like Rin Tin Tin and save his master. The ending of the original novel is bleak as the mutated humans inherit the earth. In this movie some people manage to escape and set up a kind of Christian survivor's colony somewhere in Vermont, because the virus doesn't do well in cold climates. Canadians can take heart at this news.

Surprisingly, *I Am Legend* is not a complete waste of time. There are a few strong scenes and suspenseful moments, and Will Smith is quite good. But in the hands of a different director and a different screenwriter, this could have been a significantly better film. Rent this if you must, but by all means read Matheson's book. It is a short novel, a gripping read, and it deserved better. Strike three.

Inland Empire

Are We There Yet?

(2006)

Q: How many David Lynchs does it take to change a light bulb?

A: Don't bother changing the light bulb; Mr. Lynch likes the room dark.

Even by Lynchian standards, *Inland Empire* is a bizarre, fragmented, and ultimately opaque viewing experience. About twenty minutes in, I did not know when the events were taking place or even *if* the events were really taking place. I did not have a clue about what was happening to Laura Dern's character—was she hallucinating, remembering, had she fallen down a rabbit hole, or had Dr. McCoy given her a shot of Cordrazine?

Okay, that last one is stretching it—this movie has no connection to *Star Trek*—but for all of the sense that it makes, which is to say none at all, it might as well be happening in that parallel universe where the Enterprise gang was turned into a bunch of pirates and Spock had a beard. In other words, *Inland Empire* feels very much as if Lynch made it up as he went along—and he may well have. When the movie began filming, there was no script. Lynch's modus operandi for *Inland Empire* was to shoot little bits of ideas when they came to him and to later assemble these bits with an eye on creating a coherent whole.

Unfortunately, rather than a coherent whole, what he has created seems more like an incoherent (black) hole. As a film reviewer who has had to sit through my share of nonsensical movies, I don't need to tell you how extremely leery I am of directors who take off without a flight plan. Even a director as talented and inspired as David Lynch needs to have some kind of a road map if he is to avoid driving off a cliff. To compound the problem, *Inland Empire* is three hours long.

I am a fan of Lynch's films, but not an unconditional fan. He has made some brilliant, intriguing, challenging, exasperating movies, but I expect him to at least have some idea of what he's putting up on the screen. While I think that it is an act of artistic courage to delve this publicly into one's own fears, dreams, and fantasies—I have no doubt that these visions are personal ones—the resulting movie should not leave the viewer in a semicomatose state. If I was one of those long-winded, pompous critics (you know who they are!) I'd ask, "has Lynch finally and definitively lost his footing on the slippery slope of mystery and muddle and fallen into the dark rabbit hole of his own neurotic hallucinations?"

I'd have a better chance of explaining why the price of gas goes up just before every long weekend than of explaining this plot, but being fearless, here I go.

Laura Dern is a Hollywood actress named Nikki. She is on the shortlist to obtain a part in a new film called *On High in Blue Tomorrows*. One afternoon while she is at home a woman comes to the door, a stranger, and introduces herself as a new neighbour. Nikki invites the woman in for tea. They sit down and the woman, who has a thick eastern European accent, begins to speak in riddles making increasingly enigmatic and even vaguely threatening comments like, "Actions have consequences; you have forgotten to pay a bill." At this point, and remember that we are only a few minutes into the film, I started to laugh because I knew that Lynch was putting me on. This character is the Lynchian equivalent of Maria Ouspenskaya telling Lon Chaney in *The Wolfman*, "Beware the full moon, when the wolf bane blooms." Lynch loves to set up so-called mysteries that lead absolutely nowhere because he knows that audiences can't resist a mystery. And I think that he is also a bit of a sadist. You would have to be to lead the audience around in circles for three hours with no payoff in the end.

Later, Nikki meets with her new director (portrayed by

Jeremy Irons) and she is told that the movie they will be making is a remake of a Polish film that was never completed because the main actors were murdered (!). Lynch throws us another bone by delivering a murder mystery. He also throws in a violently jealous husband, a costar who is notorious for having affairs with his leading ladies, and a prostitute who is seen several times watching television in a hotel room. What she is watching is a deeply weird sitcom that features giant, anthropomorphic rabbits who say things like, "I have a secret" and "It won't turn out the way you think" while a seemingly random laugh track is heard in the background. At other times an off-camera studio audience is heard applauding and cheering for no discernible reason.

Giant rabbits. I'm not kidding.

And if that weren't enough, add to the mix a woman who is either insane or hypnotized and who carries a screwdriver (that she is supposed to kill someone with), plus (just for good measure, and why the heck not at this point) throw in some gratuitous nudity and a group of Hollywood prostitutes who launch into a choreography to the tune of "The Locomotion" and you have a recipe for . . . what exactly? The last thing David Lynch is concerned with is telling us a conventional story. What is he thinking? Why has he made this movie, who does he think the target audience is composed of, and what in the name of the Easter Bunny is that sitcom all about?

Lynch discussed his methods in a 1996 interview published in *Kinorevue* in Czechoslovakia:

A film consists of many parts, which are all of the same importance, I believe. Sometimes the visual imagination leads to a change in part of the story. At other times the story leads to visual creation. It works both ways, everything flows together. There are no rules, but in the end all the parts must fit together precisely. That is the only way to create something interesting.

Inland Empire was financed by Studio Canal in France and by a group of Polish investors. It is not a movie that would ever have received significant production money in the States because American film producers are extremely wary of (read: allergic to) movies that defy description. And not only does *Inland Empire* defy description, but the act of sitting through it is a major chore. It is such a chore, in fact, that it could be a particularly nasty initiation rite for new students entering a film study course at university. If you are not a Lynch fan, you should avoid this at all costs because it overflows with the worst excesses of Lynch's oeuvre. If you've never seen a Lynch film, this is not the one to start with. Allow me instead to recommend *Blue Velvet*, a disturbing piece of twisted Americana, or *Mulholland Drive*, which also makes very little sense, but is positively crystal clear in comparison to *Inland Empire*. It is also much, much more entertaining.

All of this being said, and as hopelessly muddled as *Inland Empire* is, Lynch is raising some very pertinent points about how contemporary Western societies are obsessed with images and image making, and how individual and collective identity becomes fragmented in a culture saturated by media. Lynch is announcing, in his own inimitable fashion, the demise of the Hollywood image-making machine, now that technology has given everyone the opportunity to make a movie (*Inland Empire* was shot using a relatively inexpensive hand-held digital camera). Hollywood is a fallen empire that is no longer the prime generator of fantasy for mass consumption. Technology has been democratized, and anyone can create and consume a movie and put his or her own inland empire on display.

But please, write a script first.

Inland Empire reheats (or revisits) all of the major themes explored in *Mulholland Drive* but with much less clarity. But even as messy as it is, *Inland Empire* still manages some moments of brilliance. Of course if you drop as many bombs as this movie does, intellectually and philosophically speaking, you are bound to hit something.

A word should be said about Laura Dern who is outstanding here. I doubt very much that she had any idea what Lynch was directing her to do and why, but she gives a powerful performance as a character completely overwhelmed by the events unfolding around her. Perhaps she wasn't acting.

In the end, I see *Inland Empire* as more of a performance piece than a traditional film. I don't think that it should be shown in a traditional movie theatre with traditional show times. The way to see this, I think, would be to have it playing all day long in a dark, empty room, and people could wander in and out and watch the film in bits and pieces to get what they can from it. It's not really a movie in the traditional sense at all; it's more like an experimental video installation in an art gallery.

There is an appetite out there for movies that couldn't care less about focus groups and the bottom line. I am glad that David Lynch is able to make movies like *Inland Empire*, and I feel that it does have artistic merit, but there will be accusations of self-indulgence. To answer the question of which audience Lynch had in mind for this, I think that, like all true artists, Lynch makes his work for himself; if it happens to strike a chord with others, so be it, and if not, tough. This movie is an artistic statement—a very messy artistic statement, but still—and so deeply personal, so filled with Lynch's own demons, that most audiences will find it impossible to connect with it. Approach at your own risk.

The Last Airbender

(2010)

I will never again review a film directed by M. Night Shyamalan unless he gets someone else to write the screenplay; I just can't stand it anymore.
—Robert Fontaine, CBC Radio, 2008

Q: Why did I decide to review *The Last Airbender* only two years after I was so exasperated by M. Night Shyamalan's *The Happening*?

A: *The Last Airbender* is based on an award-wining Nickelodeon animated television series called *Avatar: The Last Airbender*, which ran from 2005 to 2008. I believed, naively as it turns out, that because this was based on material from another medium (i.e., material that Shyamalan had not written), it might not be lost in the Bermuda Triangle of rotten writing that has claimed so many of Shyamalan's films. I have to admit, however, that after seeing the trailer, I thought that *The Last Airbender* had a real chance of being Shyamalan's masterpiece of ineptitude. For a film reviewer, there is a morbid kind of fascination at play when you know — you just *know* — that a movie has the potential of being the cinematic equivalent of a caramel and baloney sandwich. It's like being offered front row seats for a train wreck; you feel guilty as hell, but how can you not look?

In *The Last Airbender* the world is divided into four kingdoms: Water, Air, Earth, and Fire. The world has been at peace under the supervision of an Avatar, a link to the spirit world and the only being capable of mastering the use of all four elements. When the young Avatar Aang disappears, the Fire Nation launches an attack to eradicate all members of the Air Nomads to prevent interference in their future plans for world domination.

Critic's note: You were afraid something like this would happen, weren't you?

One hundred years pass and the current Fire Lord Ozai continues to conquer and imprison anyone with elemental bending abilities in the Earth and Water Kingdoms. One day siblings Katara and Sokka, who belong to a Southern Water Tribe, find a mysterious boy trapped beneath the ice outside their village. He reveals himself to be Aang, an Avatar and the last of the Air Nomads. Swearing allegiance, Katara and Sokka journey with him to the Northern Water Kingdom in his quest to master waterbending and eventually fulfill his destiny of once again restoring peace to the world. But as they approach their goal, they must evade Prince Zuko and the tyrannical onslaught of the evil Fire Lord himself.

As far as the boy being mysterious; we know immediately that he is the chosen one. Let's face it; when you find a boy frozen in a block of ice who has a shaved head and esoteric tattoos on his skull, you just know this is not the newspaper delivery boy who went missing last winter.

From the moment we were first introduced to Katara and Sokka in the arctic regions of their water kingdom, I knew the audience was in big trouble. Why? Because the 3D effect is astonishingly awful—the actors look like cardboard stand-ups in a video store. This isn't just your ordinary, everyday cheesy 3D; *The Last Airbender* appears to have been shot in Spectacular Widescreen Crummy-Vision. When reviewing *Clash of the Titans* in 2010, I called it the worst 3D ever—and it was, up to that point—but this one is going to the Crummy 3D Hall of Fame. And the cinema charges you an extra three dollars for this junk.

The *noive*.

If the Avatar ruled in the real world, the cinemas would be forced to give you a three dollar discount for having to watch this. But as bad as the 3D is, the special effects are dreadful. This is a serious problem for a film that is almost all special effects. The best effect I experienced during *The Last Airbender* was the air conditioning in the theatre.

The dialogue is up to par with the 3D and the effects: it consists almost exclusively of the characters explaining to each other what is going on, or else it is absurdly stilted, as in, "we must journey to the far reaches in order to liberate the people from the tyranny of the Fire Nation! Shall we go now? Yes . . . let's!"

Dev Patel, the young star of *Slumdog Millionnaire*, portrays the young and desperate-to-please-his-father Prince Zuko. He gives an acceptable performance considering the totally insipid dialogue he has to spout. Noah Ringer portrays the young Avatar Aang. This is his first screen role (he is the voice of the character Aang in the video-game version). What is mostly required of him is that he look really earnest and make a lot of silly kung-fu type moves while the lousy special effects have him bending air or water. The script should have had him learning to throw a knuckleball. At least that would have been interesting.

But as poorly constructed and wobbly as this movie rollercoaster is, the real chills and thrills come from the ineptitude of the teenage actors who portray Katara and Sokka, Nicola Peltz and Jackson Rathbone (Jasper Hale of *Twilight Saga* fame). Both of them seem to be in over their heads, but Rathbone is particularly unconvincing.

This is critic-speak for a plush toy would have been more believable.

To be fair, no one seems to have received any real direction, or rather the young actors seem to have received direction like "pretend you're in grade three and you are in the Christmas show" or "you're wearing this really cool costume and you're going trick or treating . . . stay in character!"

I would never say that this is the worst movie I have ever

seen—there is no such animal, there are so many—but it has to be close. After sitting through *The Last Airbender*, my feelings about M. Night Shyamalan are simple: I think that there is as much chance of him making a solid and engaging film in the future as there is of my dog, Buffie, sitting down at the piano and playing a Dave Brubeck tune.

Lincoln Lawyer

(2011)

Mathew McConaughey portrays Mickey Haller, a sleazy, street-savvy lawyer who conducts a very lucrative business out of the back of his big, black Lincoln Town Car. Well, why not? Have you seen what decent office space costs these days?

WE INTERRUPT THIS REVIEW TO BRING YOU SOME
HISTORICAL CONTEXT:

I need to say a few things about Perry Mason. For those of you under the age of fifty, let me explain that Perry Mason is not the inventor of those really useful jars, but rather a character in a long series of hugely popular crime novels written by Earle Stanley Gardner and published over four decades beginning in the 1930s. The character of Perry Mason was so popular that he appeared in various Hollywood films in the thirties and forties; he eventually got his own radio series and with the advent of television, a long-running and enormously successful television series, which ran from 1957 to 1966. The show featured Raymond Burr as the L.A. defence attorney who always defended innocent people and who always found a way of not only getting his clients exonerated but also of finding the real murderer. His foil, week in and week out, was the long-suffering district attorney Hamilton Burger who never won a case. By the time the show went off the air, the final score was Mason 271, Burger 0.

Ouch. Even Charlie Brown never lost that many ball games.

I always thought it was rather funny and cruel that the poor sap was named Hamilton Burger, because hamburger is what good old

Perry turned him into every week. Near the end of each episode, when Perry would wring a confession out of the real murderer or present (with much theatricality) some surprise piece of evidence that exonerated his client, poor Hamilton's eyes would bulge, and he would gnash his teeth, and beads of sweat would appear on his forehead. I never felt sorry for him.

AND NOW BACK TO OUR REVIEW, ALREADY IN PROGRESS:

Like *Perry Mason*, *Lincoln Lawyer* is also set in L.A., and it bears obvious similarities to the classic TV show. It is in fact a kind of hip, contemporary take on Perry Mason. Think Perry Mason in a car. You older folks might remember that when the Perry Mason series finally ran its course, CBS found a way to resurrect Raymond Burr's career by putting him on wheels as *Ironside*, a wheelchair-bound private detective. So what we have here is a bit of a mash up; a Perry Masonish character in a Lincoln Continental. As contrived and silly as this may sound, McConaughey's enthusiasm turns the movie into a pretty cool ride, and he is obviously having fun with the tough, cynical lines his character gets to toss around, as when he tells a potential informant, "I checked the list of people I trust and your name ain't on it." This kind of snappy reply would not be out of place coming from the mouth of Bogart's Sam Spade.

If you have a big, black car fetish—and with all of the weirdness on the Internet now, I'll bet there are at least three sites devoted to that—*Lincoln Lawyer* will certainly shift your gears. The movie offers lots of scenes of this big, black Lincoln Town Car turning corners and coming to smooth-as-silk stops in front of the county courthouse. McConaughey may be the star of the movie, but the car gets the sexiest close-ups.

To continue with my Perry Mason angle; not only does our very slick lawyer Mickey have a chauffeur named Earl, but Mick also has a young secretary named Lorna, and an investigator and right-hand man named Frank (William H. Macy). Perry Mason had a secretary named Della Street (Barbara Hale) and an investigator named Paul (William Hopper).

When it comes to clients, Mickey isn't choosy: bikers, con artists, drunk drivers, drug dealers, you name it. Whereas Perry Mason would only defend you if he thought you were innocent, we understand that Mickey Haller would defend Darth Vader if Darth could afford him. One day a young Beverly Hills playboy named Louis Roulet (Ryan Phillippe) is arrested and accused of viciously assaulting a woman he picked up in a bar. He asks specifically for Haller to defend him. Roulet has a very rich mother, and Mickey's eyes light up like a pinball machine in anticipation of the ridiculous fee he is going to charge to get this kid off the hook. And as the case begins to unfold, it looks like a cakewalk. But then Mickey's associate is murdered, and he realizes that the case is not as it seemed. Events are precipitated from that point on, and the film morphs into an engrossing courtroom drama as Mickey is placed in the difficult position of defending a case that he really wants to lose.

In the early going, *Lincoln Lawyer* is a first-rate suspense thriller, a solid whodunit. After watching McConaughey sleepwalk through some pretty bad movies in recent years, it's nice to see him put some enthusiasm and energy into a role, and *Lincoln Lawyer* turns out to be a very good vehicle (sorry!) for him. Terrific casting also elevates the proceedings with Marisa Tomei particularly good as Mickey's sharp-as-a-tack ex-wife who also happens to be a district attorney. I don't know how plausible it would be for a defence attorney to be married to a D.A. if both were trying cases in the same jurisdiction, but I would imagine that the sparks would fly and there is some very good give and take between Tomei and McConaughey. William H. Macy is (of course) solid and great fun to watch as the investigator, and I loved his 1967-era Jefferson Airplane hairdo. Ryan Phillippe is also good as the sleazy and perhaps sociopathic young man accused of the heinous crime. Even the small roles are perfectly cast, with Laurence Mason as the driver Earl giving an excellent performance. John Leguizamo walks the walk as a sleazy acolyte of our sleazy hero.

As you can see, there's a whole lotta sleazy goin' on in this one.

What doesn't work here—and I haven't read the novel so I don't know if all of these plot twists and false endings are the creation of the screenwriter, John Romano—is that the plot has more rebounds than Kareem Abdul-Jabbar. Clocking in at a little under two hours, *Lincoln Lawyer* presents us with no less than three different endings, almost as if three alternate endings had been shot and no one could decide which one to use. Mixing my basketball and baseball metaphors, I would say that the script reminded me of a nervous hitter trying to do too much. By the end, my suspenders of disbelief were stretched to the breaking point.

Lincoln Lawyer is an entertaining film, although it feels more like a high-quality TV show. This is the kind of cool but ultimately silly premise that you can only really get away with on television. How could this possibly work in real life? Just think about the traffic in L.A., and the fact that lawyers have to be on time and have tons of deadlines, and the price of driving around in a 1980s Lincoln Town Car all day—the thing gets about ten miles to the gallon—it would be cheaper to have a proper office. But on TV, stuff like this has never mattered, and never will. Like it doesn't matter that on *Murder, She Wrote* the little Maine village of Cabot Cove has a murder rate ten times that of Detroit. Or that Mr. and Mrs. Howell and Ginger on *Gilligan's Island* went for a three-hour cruise with seventy-two trunks of clothing. It was the weight of the Howell's wardrobe that sank the Minnow! *Lincoln Lawyer* moves along sharply, like a fine automobile, gliding smoothly over its numerous plot holes, and it gives you some bang for your dollar. Not a bad deal these days.

Match Point

(2005)

Woody Allen has written and directed several movies that rank among the very best produced anywhere in the world over the course of the last forty-five years. *Match Point* presents a paradox—in some ways it is a departure for Allen, but it also revisits some of his earlier work.

Woody (I feel that I've earned the right to call him that; I've spent enough hours watching his movies) has never been a formulaic filmmaker. I suppose that his films can be grouped into comedies and dramas, although his best films contain elements of both genres. *Match Point* is one of the most serious films he has made—it is almost straight drama—but before anyone runs for cover, let me say that this has nothing to do with the dark and dreary films he made when he was channelling Bergman several years ago.

Woody has sometimes made what I call identity-crisis films: *Interiors* (which I hated), *Shadows and Fog*, and *September*. His deep love and respect for Bergman's films, and his desire to make more serious films undoubtedly motivated him—even comic geniuses can occasionally stumble over the ridiculous yet widely held argument that straight drama is somehow more artistic than comedy—but the aforementioned movies felt rather forced, overly serious, and angst ridden. *Match Point* is much closer to *Crimes and Misdemeanors*, which I still consider to be his finest film. Not only are the explored themes in the two films almost identical, but the narrative and cinematic means he employs are also very close. The major difference between *Match Point* and *Crimes and Misdemeanors* is that the former lacks the humorous counterpoint that lightened up the plot in the latter. *Match Point* is deadly serious, and it is riveting.

At one hundred and twenty-four minutes, *Match Point* is also longer than any previous Woody Allen movie — he deserves a lifetime achievement award for brevity. Time being a most precious commodity, I can't tell you how much I appreciate a director who can tell a story in ninety minutes or less. Quite simply, most two-hour movies are about twenty minutes too long. I was at first surprised that he had made a film this long, but then it occurred to me that movies in general have been getting longer over the course of the past twenty years. The ninety-minute movie is no longer considered the commercial standard that it was back in the sixties, seventies, and eighties when double features were still the norm in cinemas. And over the course of his long career, Woody has gone from making movies primarily with American audiences in mind to making movies for the European market, where critical and commercial reception has been consistently more positive. The spectacular bumps in his personal life have also had a negative impact on his commercial viability in the United States. It was only a matter of time before he packed up and decided to make his films in places like England, France, and Italy where he could more easily obtain funding — his European films serve as gorgeous travel brochures for American audiences — and where his personal life was not a commercial liability.

For the first ninety minutes, *Match Point* presents a delectable mélange of psychological character study and romantic drama. It then smoothly and slyly shifts gears and becomes a murder thriller vaguely reminiscent of Hitchcock and even — dare I say her name? — Agatha Christie. And it all works beautifully.

Warning: If you want to see this movie cold (i.e., without knowing anything at all about it), then you're probably not even reading this right now, so who the heck am I talking to?

The major theme of *Match Point* is that luck plays a deciding role in human affairs. Woody has stated, "I've been incredibly lucky. People have a tendency to underplay the role of luck in life and I feel that people underplay that because they're so scared to lose control. I don't feel that."

The film opens with a shot of a tennis court. A ball is being hit back and forth, and the narrator tells us that it is now match point. The ball is hit and the camera freezes the ball in space above the net. The narrator tells us that luck will now intervene, and two things are possible: the ball will either fall back on the side of the server and he or she will lose the game, or the ball will fall over the net and the server will win. Lucky or unlucky?

In *Match Point*, Allen also explores other themes that have been near and dear to his heart over the years, including ruminating on the moral structure of the universe, and searching for justice, temporal or otherwise. *Match Point* is his most philosophically substantial film since *Crimes and Misdemeanors*, and references to Dostoevsky's *Crime and Punishment* are sprinkled throughout. Without getting into that major work of literature, suffice it to say that even a cursory glance at the Cole's Notes would reveal Allen's script enthusiastically channelling Dostoevsky.

— — —

Plot: *Match Point* is constructed along the lines of a classic English social melodrama, where a social climber, rising above his or her humble origins, is eventually undone by an excess of ambition or an unfortunate turn of events. Reworking the traditional form — as he did in *Crimes and Misdemeanors* — Allen (and Lady Luck) ultimately favours the villain.

A young, good-looking Irish professional tennis player named Chris (Jonathan Rhys Myers) has a job interview at a posh, very exclusive London tennis club. We learn that he has had enough of the pro circuit; he has done all right but he will never be a top player, and he is now interested in a career as a tennis instructor. He is hired and quickly makes friends with a young man named Terry who comes from a very rich family. They soon discover that they share a love of opera, and Terry (who has great tickets) invites him to a performance.

I was immediately suspicious of Chris. Did he really like opera? Of course, I'm suspicious when anyone says they love opera.

We later see Chris at home reading *Crime and Punishment* and a book on Dostoevsky. Chris seems to be cramming for an exam. It becomes obvious that he feels that opera and Dostoevsky are going to help him enter the inner circle of Terry's family and aid his social ambitions. Quite soon, he becomes romantically involved with Terry's sister Chloe, who falls head over heels for him. One day at a family gathering while playing a game of table tennis, Chris makes a pass at Terry's fiancée, Nola (Scarlett Johansson). In this scene his true nature is revealed: Chris is without scruples. He wants to get ahead in the world, and he is going to manipulate those who trust him by charming people—into bed, or marriage even—for his financial benefit. It doesn't take long before Chris marries Chloe and he begins a torrid affair with Nola. And as is the case in *Crimes and Misdemeanors*—when Martin Landau's character is caught ever more tightly in the grasp of his mistress—the married man will turn in desperation to murder to extricate himself.

— — —

Match Point presents us with a richly textured scenario. Woody's script is one of his best—it deservedly received an Oscar nomination for Best Original Screenplay—and it avoids getting tangled in its multiple dramatic threads, moving along smartly as it visits various moral and philosophical points of interest while always keeping the audience guessing. And like many, if not all, of Woody's best films, it must be interpreted as a cautionary tale. Woody is restating some points that have been central to many of his plots: beware not only of what you wish for, but of what you may be willing to do to keep your position. And even if you escape in the temporal world, can you ever run away from yourself?

Alcohol, often a favourite prop or device in Allen's movies, becomes almost a character unto itself in *Match Point*—a mischievous gremlin that makes the characters lose not only their inhibitions, but also their sense of right and wrong. In many scenes the consumption of alcohol is the catalyst for dramatic events as characters say things they shouldn't, confess things they should keep quiet, and do things they will regret later. Is alcohol just a convenient dramatic device, or is Allen saying something more profound about the champagne- and gin-soaked upper crust? Why do these people drink so much? The easy, flippant answer is because they can afford to. But this is also a portrait of alcohol as the root of evil, a symptom of spiritual emptiness and existential boredom, a crutch, and an excuse for failure.

Film students take note: A thesis could be written on Woody Allen's use of alcohol; I don't mean in his personal life, I mean in his screenplays. And in *Match Point*, red wine takes on a symbolic significance. Biblical references occur in many of Allen's films (an obvious example is the name of Martin Landau's character in *Crimes and Misdemeanors*, Judas) and in *Match Point* the screenplay has Chris (from the Greek *Christos*—the Christ, Anointed One) being visited by the ghosts of his victims and then knocking over a glass of red wine—symbolically spilling blood for his own material gain.

At the beginning of *Match Point* a tennis ball hits the top of a net and we are left to wonder which way it will fall. Near the end of the film, a similar occurrence will determine the outcome of the dramatic events. But the audience must consider the following point, which is, I think, the real match point: has the protagonist really won, or have his worst fears been realized? This question harks back to *Crimes and Misdemeanors*, although in that one Martin Landau's character was able to liberate himself from the pangs of his conscience and get on with his life. Chris in *Match Point* is not so lucky. The final image we see of his face is chilling: a man fully conscious of the horror he has perpetrated, trapped within himself with no exit and no hope of salvation.

Moneyball

(2011)

Something weird and totally unexpected happened in Oakland in 2002: the Oakland A's baseball team surprised everyone—well, almost everyone—by making it to the American League Championship Series. Even though they lost to the Yankees in the end, it was a remarkable achievement. Only a few months earlier, A's fans were crushed by the loss of their three best players to the Yankees and the Boston Red Sox. Oakland general manager, Billy Beane, had been faced with the seemingly impossible task of rebuilding a team and making it competitive with very little money. *Moneyball* is the story of how he did it, and how he put a new spin on statistical analysis in baseball.

I can hear some of you right now. Oh wow. A movie about statistical analysis in baseball . . . whoopee! What a thrilling concept for a big-budget Hollywood movie; why didn't anyone think of this before? I just can't wait to see all those computer graphics and flow charts and exciting close-ups of Brad Pitt's fingers flying across his laptop as he calculates the WHIP (walks plus hits per inning pitched) of the two pitchers he's trying to trade for.

What makes this movie truly exciting is that it not only has Pitt calculating WHIP on his laptop, but also wheeling and dealing over the phone while scarfing down a Twinkie. You want to talk about multitasking? I'm pooped just thinking about it.

— — —

When I heard that someone wanted to make a film of Michael Lewis' book *Moneyball: The Art of Winning an Unfair Game*, I thought that it would surely be a documentary. I could see baseball nerds like myself running out to a repertory cinema to see a documentary about this, but not in a million years would I have imagined that it could be turned into a big-budget Hollywood movie featuring a big-name star—but then I didn't think that the story of Facebook could ever be a popular movie either. In fact, *Moneyball* is written by Aaron Sorkin, the same screenwriter who wrote *The Social Network*. For *Moneyball*, Sorkin inherited a script that had been previously developed by Steve Soderbergh—the director first attached to the project. True to his style, Soderbergh's script was a much more complex affair; a multi-layered story that would have blended fiction and documentary. This final version of *Moneyball* is directed by Bennett Miller, who directed *Capote*.

On the surface, it might seem like quite a stretch to compare writer Truman Capote to baseball manager Billy Beane. But if we look closer we see two free thinkers, characters who dared to think way outside the box in order to achieve success. Capote pioneered a new literary form, the non-fiction novel *In Cold Blood*, while Beane pioneered a new way of evaluating a ball player's true value on the field. As Capote's book was hugely influential in the literary field, so were Beane's ideas hugely influential on the ball field. His 2002 Oakland A's became the prototype and the proving ground for a statistical approach that many major league teams eventually adopted, often with greater success than Beane himself achieved.

The screenwriter, Sorkin, has very deftly refocused Lewis' original book. Had he not, most moviegoers would have found *Moneyball* about as riveting as a rain delay. With the exception of rabid baseball fans—and I'm talking foaming at the mouth here—people simply will not flock to a movie that involves characters having heated discussions about the relative merits of on-base percentage versus runs batted in. But they might flock to a movie that has Brad Pitt having heated discussions about on-base percentage versus runs batted in while scarfing down a Twinkie, overturning a table in frustration, and fielding a call from his ex-wife who is worried about their fourteen-year-old daughter.

Big difference.

By focusing on the human dimension of the story, and by setting it up in terms of conflict—Beane's crafty David versus the Goliath of traditional baseball thinking—Sorkin presents something that even non-baseball fans can cheer for. Everybody loves an underdog, and Billy Beane becomes an almost iconic figure. After all, he represents everyone who ever dared tell the boss that they were wrong; that there is a better way if only we would abandon dogma.

No matter what kind of story you are telling—about baseball, flu epidemics, or social networking—you have to make it compelling. And the way to make it compelling is to set up a conflict, some challenge that the hero must overcome. And of course it helps if you can heavily stack the odds against your hero and surround him with people who are not only skeptical of his ideas, but positively hostile to every word that comes out of his mouth. Early on in *Moneyball*, there is a terrific scene that really brings all of these elements together. General manager Billy Beane is having a big strategy session with his top baseball people. The group includes several old-school scouts—who might have been named Crusty, Dusty, and Musty, had this been an animated cartoon—and they have been doing this, they remind Billy, "for a hundred years, and goddamn it, we know how to judge baseball talent and we know which young players are going to be successful." But of course, they don't. They are just mucking about like they always have.

This scene hilariously exposes much of the voodoo analysis and the hocus pocus that has been at work in baseball since its earliest days. Enter Peter (Jonah Hill), a nerdish-looking kid who doesn't know anything about baseball but has a degree in economics from Stanford. The kid announces that most baseball experts "aren't looking at the right stats." Beane has hired Peter as a special assistant, and the kid is about to severely alienate Crusty, Dusty, and Musty—Beane's mummified scouts.

So, there is a big chart on the wall with dozens of names of minor leaguers, of major league free agents, and of prospects and has-beens. Names get tossed around at a furious pace. "Okay, Phil, who do you like?" asks Billy. "You know, Billy, I really like this kid Granelli," Phil replies. Another scout pipes up, "yeah, he looks really good; the kid has great style, Billy, a great swing, and he *looks* like a ball player. Great face."

Great face?

Face is important. Well, it used to be. Back in the old days, several baseball insiders seriously suggested that Yogi Berra would never make it with the Yankees because he was too odd-looking. Of course, sometimes picking a player is a no-brainer. Back in the 1930s, the Cleveland Indians signed Bob Feller when he was only seventeen years old because he was a big strong kid who could throw a baseball through a brick wall—no-brainer. But when trying to evaluate an average player (which the great majority of players are), how can you tell which one could help your team? Well, if you really knew their strengths and weaknesses, and if you had numbers that really meant something, it would give you a marked advantage.

Baseball has had statistics forever, but which ones are significant? Some statistics that had been formerly overlooked are now known to be highly significant in determining a player's value.

Back to our baseball meeting.

Beane says, "Yeah, Phil, the kid looks good, but his on-base percentage is terrible, 200. Who else have you got? What about Jiminez?" One of the scouts looks up and says, totally serious, "Jiminez has an ugly girlfriend . . . you know? That shows low self-esteem; we don't want a kid like that." This is both funny and pathetic, but this is what Beane was up against—the old-school voodoo.

The Oakland manager that year was Art Howe, played here with gruff understatement by Philip Seymour Hoffman sporting a buzz cut. Howe thought that Beane was crazy. He would have preferred to eat pine tar than follow Beane's direction. And early in the season, the team lost, and lost, and lost some more. The film gives us a wonderful sports movie montage of the team losing and the fans screaming for Beane's head on a platter. The irony of the whole thing is that when the team finally did start to win (and win, and win some more) Howe received credit in the media for his managerial skills. In reality, he was fighting Beane all the way. I won't say that Hoffman's very considerable acting skills are wasted exactly, but his screen time is limited—a small but important role that could have been greatly expanded.

As effective as *Moneyball* is, the narrative flow suffers from a surfeit of flashbacks. We flash back to Billy Beane's own failed career as a promising prospect, deciding to sign with the Mets instead of going on to college. There are many close-ups of family pictures, and Pitt spends a lot of time staring earnestly off into space. Mind you, Pitt does this as well as any actor out there, but this is a lot of staring and head hanging. There is excellent chemistry between Pitt and Jonah Hill as his nerdy statistician. Both Pitt and Hill were nominated for Oscars, and they bounce so smartly off each other that both performances are elevated. Brad Pitt fans will also love it—it is a strong, though not a great, performance. I think that in years to come, this will become a baseball classic along the lines of *Bull Durham* and *Eight Men Out*. Unfortunately, however, the profound significance of walks plus hits per inning pitched (WHIP) will be totally lost on most moviegoers who would undoubtedly be more excited by seeing Brad Pitt wielding the other kind of whip.

Baseball fans will enjoy *Moneyball*. Other interested groups would include statisticians, business analysts, sociologists, and lawn-care specialists. Wally Pfister's cinematography captures the irresistibly cinematic *je ne sais quoi* that is evoked by an impeccably manicured outfield and sprinklers going full tilt in the soft summer twilight. A baseball field is a beautiful thing, and in this case, magnificent on a big screen.

My Week with Marilyn

(2011)

If you are ever introduced to someone as "the immortal so-and-so," you will undoubtedly be wearing wings and attending a meet and greet at Saint Peter's Bar & Grill. Immortality is not for the living. Marilyn Monroe inhabits the upper golden spheres of Celebrity Valhalla—a person so famous that sometimes it seems as if she must be a figment of the collective cultural imagination.

In 1976 (when Marilyn would have turned fifty) the award-wining novelist Larry McMurtry, who wrote *Terms of Endearment* and who also cowrote the screenplay for *Brokeback Mountain*, wrote a piece in the *New York Times*. In it he said, "she is right in there with our major ghosts: Hemingway, the Kennedy brothers—people who finished with American life before America had time to finish with them." Well, the Kennedys didn't have much choice in the matter, someone else finished it for them; and Hemingway committed suicide as did Marilyn—although the conspiracy theorists will never leave it alone, and I can understand why. It's extremely difficult for many people to accept that someone so physically beautiful and so incredibly famous could decide that life wasn't worth living. All that the public sees are the outward trappings of fame. No one knows how it feels on the inside.

My Week with Marilyn is based on the memoir of the same name written by Colin Clark and published in 1995. In 1956, Clark was a twenty-three-year-old aspiring film director. He wasn't quite sure if he wanted to direct, but he was certain that he wanted to be involved in the movies. He came from a rich family. His father was a world-renowned art historian who counted Sir Laurence Olivier and wife Vivien Leigh among his friends. So, as a favour to his friend, Sir Laurence (portrayed here by Kenneth

Branagh) gave the young man a job as third assistant director on the new film he was directing and producing, tentatively titled *The Sleeping Prince*. It would eventually be released as *The Prince and the Showgirl*. Olivier had enlisted no less than Marilyn Monroe to star opposite him. It was a surprising pairing; the celebrated stage actor, one of the brilliant actors of his time, with the celebrated movie star who was studying the method with Lee and Paula Strasberg in New York. When the production began, there was friction between Sir Laurence and Marilyn, and pretty soon after, combustion.

━ ━ ━

Plot: It's the summer of 1956. Sir Laurence Olivier has become interested in the Marilyn phenomenon—the dean of British actors may be a little star struck himself—and he has decided to combine their talents in a romantic comedy that he feels will be a certain box-office success. The film will shoot in England, and our young hero Colin (Eddie Redmayne) scores points with Olivier right from the start when he finds a suitably secluded house for Marilyn (Michelle Williams) and her entourage. Colin quickly gains Olivier's confidence. As third director he is really just Olivier's gopher, but Olivier opens up to him in ways that he can't with others. Colin finds himself in a privileged position to observe events on and off the set. Marilyn shows up late every day, unable to remember her lines; her acting coach, Paula Strasberg, appears to be glued to her, contesting Olivier's direction at every turn. "Marilyn isn't ready," she tells him, "she has to get into character." Olivier huffs and puffs and declares that "teaching that girl to act . . . it would be easier to teach Urdu to a badger!" And this is just the beginning.

Marilyn is insecure, riddled with self-doubt about her own talent. She is terrified of Olivier who is really quite mean to her. After Olivier has vociferously criticized Marilyn, another member of the cast Dame Sybil (Judi Dench)—who we have been led to believe is a bit of an acting snob and possibly hostile to Marilyn—sticks up for her in front of Olivier and the crew. Sybil asks him when he is going to help this "poor girl who is far from home and among strangers." She later confides to Olivier that "we may be celebrated actors and possess a lot of craft, but the only one here who knows how to act for the camera is Marilyn." Fairly quickly, seeking refuge from her insecurities, Marilyn comes to trust Colin and confide in him. Testing his loyalty, she asks him point blank, "Are you on my side or his?" By now totally besotted with the star, Colin answers, "Yours of course."

Clark's memoirs described a fleeting love affair between him and Marilyn. We can't be sure how much he embellished and what actually transpired, if anything, but the idea that the Hollywood star could have a platonic (but still emotionally intense) relationship with this young man under difficult circumstances is quite believable. Although very recently wed to playwright Arthur Miller, Monroe was having problems with her husband. In the film, Miller decides to return to New York because he isn't getting any work done. Marilyn feels alone, and we see that under her bombshell persona she is very vulnerable. She seems to be several people at once: Norma Jean the little girl lost, and the sexy and manipulative Marilyn—a mixed-up person who is slowly being destroyed by her own fame. And yet she seems addicted to the attention she receives, as if her celebrity is the only real proof that anyone loves her. Seeking escape, Marilyn decides to play hooky from the set for a few days, and Colin becomes her running mate.

The cast is very strong. In some ways Kenneth Branagh has been portraying Sir Laurence Olivier for years, even when he is portraying someone else, and he glides into this role as if slipping into a favourite bathrobe. Judi Dench as Dame Sybil Thorndike, a venerable English actress, is her usual impeccable self. Emma Watson (of Harry Potter fame) portrays a wardrobe girl who falls for the young Colin. She makes the most of her limited screen time and proves once again that she possesses great screen charisma. Her portrayal of a young girl competing hopelessly with a Hollywood icon for this young man's affections is an endearing one. Colin is well played by Eddie Redmayne. We feel his elation, confusion, and heartbreak. But the heart of the film is Michelle Williams' superb turn as Marilyn.

Michelle Williams portrayed Alma in *Brokeback Mountain*, and was nominated for an Oscar for her performance. She first impressed me in 2008 when she gave a heartbreaking, absolutely note-perfect performance in a small indie film written and directed by Kelly Reichardt called *Wendy and Lucy*, about a young homeless woman who loses her dog, Lucy. I walked out of that thinking "with the right role, this actress is going to do something great." The right role is Marilyn Monroe.

Although I haven't seen every onscreen portrayal of Marilyn, I can't imagine anyone having captured her like Michelle Williams does here. Once in a while—and not very often—I see a performance and I think, perfect. El Perfecto. But of course a movie is very much a team effort. No matter how good the actor, it is collectively the script, the direction, the set design, and the chemistry with your fellow actors that truly allow an actor to shine, to possibly be perfect. All of the elements are in place here. I did not see a better performance by an actor in 2011. Williams' performance rings true. As a film critic, I *live* for the sound of that ring.

No Country for Old Men

(2007)

If I didn't think that movies are important—that they have a
real influence on how people see and think about the world and
themselves—I wouldn't spend so much time watching them and
writing about them. Just before I reviewed *No Country for Old
Men*, I reviewed a film with Denzel Washington called *American
Gangster* that purported to tell the story of a real-life drug lord
named Frank Lucas. I had some serious problems with the moral centre of the story, or rather the lack of a moral centre. I was
not alone. *American Gangster* also raised the hackles of several
African-American columnists. Here are some of their more no-
table comments:

> *American Gangster* lifts lowlife to new heights for a gen-
> eration that doesn't remember who these people really
> were.—Elmer Smith (*Philadelphia Daily News*)

> Some knuckleheads are going to go out and see the movie
> and think that they want to be just like him.—Betty Bayé
> (*Louisville Courier-Journal*)

> Frank Lucas has been given qualities that he simply did
> not have. We see him played as a soft-spoken and sophisti-
> cated man who closely studies the written word and only
> explodes into violence every now and then. In actual-
> ity . . . Lucas was illiterate . . . [he] killed people to impress

his ruthlessness on the underworld . . . —Stanley Crouch (*New York Daily News*)

But Frank Lucas did care about his mom, or at least he does in the movie, so he wasn't all bad.

Most young people haven't seen a lot of the world—it's not their fault, I'm simply stating it as a fact—and they are in the process of discovering who they are; they look up to movie heroes, especially the based-on-a-true-story movie heroes. I think that it is at best disingenuous and probably immoral to portray real-life thugs and killers as if they were Mr. Charm, as Denzel Washington does in *American Gangster*. Call me an old stick in the mud (go on!), but I have a problem with films that glorify the worst excesses of human behaviour. And I'm glad to hear that I'm not alone.

No Country for Old Men is a brutally violent movie. It is not a film for the very young, the impressionable, or the squeamish. The violence in this movie is ugly, shocking, and disturbing. Adapting the novel by Cormac McCarthy, The Coen brothers paint an ugly portrait of a macho-crazed culture where everyone (or so it seems) is armed to the teeth, and morally and spiritually bankrupt. In this movie, America is a place where lives are disposable and violent death lurks around every corner.

The story is set in Texas in 1980 at the beginning of the Reagan years when, with old Ronnie at the wheel, America took a sharp turn to the right. The hero is a thirty-something cowboy type named Llewelyn Moss (Josh Brolin), a Vietnam vet who is out hunting one day in Texas, in the middle of nowhere near the Mexican border. Following a blood trail, he comes upon a drug deal that has gone very wrong. There are some pickup trucks in a circle and dead bodies everywhere. Everyone is dead—even a dog has been shot—and he finds the dope, which is still in a truck. He walks around and finds a dead man under a tree, and a satchel with two million dollars in it. He weighs his options for about five seconds and decides to keep the money.

Bad move.

Someone will come looking for the money. A psychotic killer (Javier Bardem), relentless and machine-like, is soon on the trail and our hero has nowhere to hide. The movie quickly turns into a long chase as our hero sends his wife (Kelly Macdonald) away to a safe place, and takes it on the lam, moving from town to town with the killer always one step behind. A parallel plot line has Tommy Lee Jones as an ageing and world-weary sheriff making a valiant attempt to get the killer before he can dispose of our hero.

Visually, *No Country for Old Men* is remarkable. Every cheesy detail, every broken-down element of junk culture—from the flea-bag motels to the dilapidated towns—is stunningly rendered by master cinematographer Roger Deakins. I was riveted by the visual style of the film while simultaneously horrified by the increasingly brutal events. Deakins has been nominated eight times for a Best Cinematography Oscar, but has never won. He was also the cinematographer on *The Assassination of Jesse James by the Coward Robert Ford* and his work on that one is breathtaking. It is ironic that such a beautiful film as *No Country for Old Men* would be filled with such horrific images. Many people die in this movie. They do not die defending noble causes or fighting for justice; they are killed mostly because the killer is insane. And they die messily and noisily, and Deakins' magical camera dwells and lingers on their deaths, and sometimes even revisits their corpses. You have been warned.

The acting is superb; the writing outstanding. The script builds nail-biting suspense and gives the audience bucket loads of action spiced up with fear, and a generous dose of that unsettling black humour that has become a trademark of the Coens. Having said all of that, I was surprised—flabbergasted would be closer to the truth—when *No Country for Old Men* won the Best Picture Oscar. Although it is supremely effective, brilliant even, I was convinced that it would die a quick (if not messy) death at the box office and go on to become a cult classic on DVD. I felt certain that a movie that takes all of the viewers' expectations and systematically blows them to smithereens could not reach a wide audience. I thought that the violence alone—brutal, disgusting, and light years removed from Tarantino faux chic—would be sufficient to turn off a majority of moviegoers and relegate the film to the out-skirts of mass popularity. At the time I first reviewed it, I said that a movie that took such obvious pleasure in robbing the audience of any shred of hope did not have a snowball's chance in hell of winning Best Picture. Not only did the film win Best Director and Best Screenplay, but it also took the Best Supporting Actor Oscar for Bardem's surreal and creepy performance—a role that should be remembered alongside such classics as Anthony Hopkins in *Silence of the Lambs*, Dennis Hopper in *Blue Velvet*, Robert Mit-chum in *Cape Fear*, and Richard Widmark in *Kiss of Death*. After the first murders, Bardem doesn't seem so much like a character as a horrific force of nature. His character becomes death incarnate.

The difference—the game-changing difference—between *American Gangster* and *No Country for Old Men* is that the latter does not dress up and choreograph its brutal violence and present the killer as some kind of cool role model. That being said, did it need to be so violent? Back in 1980, the setting for the story, this level of violence would have assured the film an X rating. In 2007 the movie was rated R. Times have changed.

No Country for Old Men sees the Coens revisiting, both sty-listically and thematically, a universe they first explored in *Fargo*, except that this time around, we aren't allowed the optimism and hope that Marge and Norm brought to the story. I fully respect the Coens for not watering down McCarthy's novel, but did *No Country for Old Men* have to be so utterly bleak? It seems to me that it would not have destroyed the spirit or the intent of the source material to allow at least Kelly Macdonald's character to live to tell the tale, but such a compromise would probably have made *No Country for Old Men* a lesser film than it is. When it comes to film, greatness is almost never the result of compromise.

See it at your own risk.

The Orphanage

A Great Horror Movie?

(2007)

So what makes a horror movie great?

Let's take one of the most analyzed, film-course discussed, dissected term-papered subjects of all time: Hitchcock's *Psycho*. *Psycho* contains many eclectic plot elements that separate it from run-of-the-mill horror. It features a doppelganger motif that has its origins in German Expressionism, and it has a preserved corpse that harkens all the way back to Grimm's fairy tales, but what makes *Psycho* so memorable is its inherent paradox. On the one hand it laid the foundation for the slasher genre, becoming one of the most imitated films of all time, while on the other hand it broke new ground by wandering into the realm of the supernatural. *Psycho* for me has always seemed more profound as a tale of possession. Norman Bates may not just have adopted the personality of his mother; he may actually be possessed by her spirit. All of the psycho-babble explanations of split personality that the doctors throw at us at the end of the film may be comforting in a sense—and Hitchcock may well have felt that a scientific explanation would connect with modern audiences increasingly aware of, and interested in, contemporary psychiatric theories—but can we be really sure that the forces compelling Norman Bates to kill aren't otherworldly?

For me, the supernatural element is crucial to the horror genre—it elevates the proceedings. Without this otherworldly element the movie may still be scary, but it seems to me that the chills are diminished if the killer is only human. What makes John Carpenter's *Halloween* so effective is that Jason is not mortal. That being said, the supernatural element is a double-edged knife. The element that makes the *Halloween* franchise so lucrative—when the bad guy is immortal you can keep bringing him back for sequels—is also what makes it ultimately predictable.

Other truly creepy films that I would recommend would be *The Haunting*, Robert Wise's 1963 film starring Julie Harris, based on the story by Shirley Jackson; *The Innocents* (1961) with Deborah Kerr as the governess plunged into an increasingly horrific situation—or is she just losing her mind?—and more recently, *The Others* (2001) with Nicole Kidman, an extremely effective and eerie film directed by Alejandro Amenábar.

Here's a secret about scary movies: they are supposed to be . . . well . . . scary. Not simply disgusting, shocking, or repulsive, as many contemporary horror films are, but they are supposed to make my spine tingle, make the hair on the back of my neck stand up, and make my heart pound. That's what a scary movie is supposed to do. If you are watching a movie and your palms don't get sweaty, then it is not a scary movie, and all the hype and marketing in the world will not make it so.

The Orphanage is produced by Guillermo Del Toro who previously directed *Pan's Labyrinth*, one of the most visually arresting films to come along in recent years, bursting with some of the most fantastic, surreal images I have seen anywhere. *The Orphanage* is directed by a first-time director, Juan Antonio Bayona. It was the highest-grossing film of 2007 in Spain and won the Best Picture award at the Barcelona Film Festival. *The Orphanage* also underlines what is severely wrong with American horror movies of the past several years. I don't think there has been a great American horror movie since Coppola's *Bram Stoker's Dracula* in 1992.

Why? Because the entire genre has degenerated. American horror films of the last fifteen years have become almost exclusively focused on the teenage market and the stories have been increasingly obsessed with sadism and psychotic behaviour. I have nothing against sadism and psychotic behaviour per se—in movies anyway—but if you throw enough straightjackets and haunted asylums and masked men with buzz saws at audiences, it all becomes ho-hum and the scripts sink under the weight of their own predictability.

In *The Orphanage*, a thirty-seven-year-old woman named Laura (Belén Rueda) returns to the orphanage where she was raised. She is returning to live there with her husband, Carlos (Fernando Cayo), and their seven-year-old son, Simón (Roger Princep). They have purchased the huge old house with the goal of turning it into a home for special needs children. Their son Simón is a cute kid, very shy, and he has a number of imaginary friends—at least his parents think they are imaginary. Strange things start to happen after Simón talks of meeting a new imaginary friend named Tomás. One day Tomás appears to Laura as a child wearing the same light blue uniform the kids wore when she was in the orphanage many years ago. This childish apparition also wears a hood over his head, like a scarecrow mask. Soon after this visitation, Simón vanishes from the house, without a trace. Laura and her husband are frantic. Where can he be? Has he perhaps been kidnapped, or is some supernatural trick being played on the family? The police investigation leads nowhere, and Laura calls in a paranormal investigator, portrayed by Geraldine Chaplin. Her investigation reveals terrible events that took place at the orphanage many years before. The plot takes the weird fork in the road.

The Orphanage borrows intelligently from several classic films, but it has its own attitude. The atmosphere created is reminiscent of *Pan's Labyrinth*—a kind of nightmarish fairy tale. *The Orphanage* also borrows story elements from *Peter Pan*, in particular the aspect of Wendy getting older but not the children. I don't want to reveal too much here, but the writer Sergio Sánchez suggests that the film can be read on two levels, like *The Innocents*: as a supernatural ghost story or as a study of a woman losing her mind. The director Juan Antonio Bayona has underlined similarities between *The Orphanage* and Roman Polanski's films *The Tenant* and *Rosemary's Baby*, although I think that the resemblances are more atmospheric than plot-based. The cinematography is beautiful, the cast superb—everything conspires effectively to make *The Orphanage* a first-rate, old-style supernatural thriller.

The Orphanage reveals itself slowly, drawing you in bit by bit—the cinematic equivalent of a hand gently tapping you on the shoulder. You turn, and there's no one there. And apart from one revolting scene, it is quite understated. I don't mean to suggest that nothing happens, plenty does, but the film doesn't rely on those silly jump moments to get you. The scene where Geraldine Chaplin's psychic is exploring the house is really creepy, although nothing really happens except that she hears strange voices. But the way that the director frames the action—the camera is always suggesting that there is something lurking just outside the frame—is highly effective and reminded me of the excellent cinematography in *The Others*.

The cast is letter perfect with Belén Rueda as Laura, a standout. A veteran Spanish character actress named Montserrat Carulla has a few scenes as a creepy old lady who is caught snooping around the house. She has a face that could stop a clock, and what happens to her is truly horrific.

The Orphanage is a little less than two hours long, and it moves along smartly. In the final ten minutes, however, there are four places where the movie could end, and it seemed to me that three of those places would have been far more effective than the ending opted for by the director—a weird yet upbeat ending, which serves to defuse the horror and suspense that it has been building to that point. Still, this is a minor quibble because the film does a terrific job of transporting its audience to some very strange places. *The Orphanage* has all the makings of a DVD cult classic; a movie seemingly designed to be watched late at night with all the lights turned off.

The Other Boleyn Girl

(2008)

While doing some historical research online, I came across this newspaper ad that appeared in the personal columns of the *Royal Tattler* in 1522.

WANTED: MISTRESS FOR MOST POWERFUL MONARCH ON EARTH. Must be young, attractive, able to bear children, and fit into size-four gowns. Rapid promotion to wife is a distinct possibility based on sexual performance and ability to connive to the top while producing male heir to the throne. This is an excellent opportunity for a dynamic, ambitious, and fecund young woman. Must be able to keep head under pressure.

Being promoted from mistress of Henry VIII to wife of Henry VIII was risky business. *The Other Boleyn Girl* is based on the bestselling novel by Philippa Gregory. It was adapted for the screen by Peter Morgan, who previously wrote the screenplay for *The Queen*, a highly entertaining film that starred Helen Mirren. I haven't read Gregory's novel, but I have it from reliable sources that its historical accuracy is rather shaky. But Hollywood has never let shaky facts stand in the way of historical drama. In Hollywood, historical dramas come in three packages: historically accurate (the rarest form), fast and loose, and not in a million years could these events have happened this way. Add a big pinch of sleaze to the latter and you have the recipe for *The Other Boleyn Girl*.

The story of Anne Boleyn has been told many times on the big screen, but never with more panache than in Hal Wallis' 1969 production of *Anne of the Thousand Days* with Geneviève

Bujold and Richard Burton. The sparks that flew between the two onscreen—Bujold was twenty-six, Burton forty-four, both were married—were ignited off screen as they had an affair that continued for several years. The French-Canadian Bujold, a fine actress, rose spectacularly to the challenge of her first Hollywood screen role by giving an Oscar-nominated performance. Unfortunately for Bujold, she was up against Maggie Smith in *The Prime of Miss Jean Brodie*. In the ensuing forty plus years, I have not seen any screen portrayal of the doomed Anne that comes close to Bujold's. It is a definitive portrait. Another fine film that explores the subject from a different angle is *A Man for All Seasons* (1966), which features a glorious performance from Paul Scofield as Sir Thomas More. The film focuses on More's moral dilemma in the face of Henry's adulterous liaison with Anne, portrayed in a brief cameo by Vanessa Redgrave. Robert Shaw, as the lusty, larger-than-life monarch, also gives a tremendous performance.

— — —

I have nothing against breathing new life into old stories, but there are limits, are there not? In rewriting history, *The Other Boleyn Girl* tries to convince us that Anne almost single-handedly orchestrated England's schism with Rome.

Pardon?

What about Cromwell? What about Cardinal Woolsey? What about any semblance of historical verisimilitude?

Historically speaking, Anne, portrayed here by Natalie Portman, was the younger Boleyn sister, Mary the eldest. In *The Other Boleyn Girl*, things get flipped around and Anne becomes the older sister. Why?

In reality, Natalie Portman is a few years older than twenty-three-year-old Scarlett Johansson who portrays Mary, but so what? Do the writers feel that it is more titillating that Henry should first bed the younger sister, get her pregnant, and then dump her for the more sophisticated older sister? Are they trying to turn this into an overblown episode of *Falcon Crest*? The comparison might seem unfair, but the entire movie exudes a television soap opera ambience that cheapens one of the most fascinating and significant periods in all of Western history. Henry, as portrayed by heart-throb Eric Bana, is reduced to a kind of desperate pawn in the love game that is orchestrated by Anne.

Give me a break.

Bana's Henry is ridiculously restrained, toothless. Robert Shaw in a straightjacket with a snorkel in his mouth would still be more formidable, not to mention believable. Shaw's Henry was blustery, lusty, vengeful—a force of nature. Richard Burton's Henry was fiery, passionate, and poetic. Physically, Bana brings a dark, matinée-idol vibe to the role, but he might as well be a pile of damp firewood for all the heat he manages to generate onscreen. Scarlett Johansson as Mary Boleyn seems terribly miscast; it's hard to believe that anyone in the sixteenth century had such a spectac-ular Botox-enhanced pout. Johansson also suffers from a debili-tating movie disease: disappearing accent. As the film progresses, she sounds less and less English and more and more American, al-though this doesn't do her any good with Henry. Natalie Portman fares a little better as Anne, but the script has her character de-veloping at a breakneck pace into an unappealing, unsympathetic, and conniving temptress. I did not like her, and by the time that she finally got shortened, I was muttering good riddance. In stark contrast, when Geneviève Bujold went to the chopping block in *Anne of the Thousand Days*, I was practically in tears.

At the heart of the sordid story, there is a scheming father and uncle trying desperately to get one of the girls into bed with the king so that they can cash in. I guess that this is a very early example of *Boleyn for Dollars*. Also prominently featured is the underhanded and occasionally histrionic rivalry between the sisters, Anne and Mary. Vying for the king's affections, Portman and Johansson be-have like cheerleaders at Hollywood High bitterly competing for the attentions of the school quarterback. Supremely insecure in its own abilities to generate real drama from the available material, the script plunges to the bottom of the melodramatic barrel to come up with the ultimate plot twist of pulp-fiction sleaze: incest. Anne herself tries to convince her brother, George, to have sex with her because she has secretly miscarried the king's child. She needs to get pregnant again without the king's knowledge.

Note to the writers responsible for *The Other Boleyn Girl*: It is *widely* accepted by historians that the accusations of incest thrown at Anne and George were completely fabricated by Cromwell in order to add weight to Anne's condemnation.

I can imagine what some of you are thinking right now. It's a movie; does it really matter if it is historically accurate? Aside from historians and snippy film critics, who really cares?

By that logic, why not take the story into the stratosphere and have Indiana Jones swing down and rescue Anne from the executioner at the last moment? Wouldn't that be even more theatrical and romantic? If the facts alone, dramatic and riveting, do not suffice to make the story worthy of a big-budget production, why not just invent a similar fictional story and go nuts with that?

Idea for aspiring screenwriters and producers: take the story of Henry VIII and Anne Boleyn and set it in a bowling alley in New Jersey. Call your movie *The Other Bowlin' Girl.* Cast Mark Wahlberg as Henry "two-door" Lazerri, the owner of The King's Lanes Bowl-O-Rama. Henry acquired his nickname "two-door" after managing his father's dilapidated used car dealership over several summers. Henry is now involved in a love triangle with two sisters, both competitive bowlers, Annie (Natalie Portman) and Mary (also Natalie Portman, in a blonde wig). Have the older sister Mary wind up in the gutter, both literally and figuratively, ruined by Henry. Have Joe Pesci portray Joey Cromwell, a mobster and owner of the cocktail lounge across the street, The Perfect Game, where Annie drinks away her frustrations over her inability to keep Wahlberg's affections. The story comes to a tragic end when Annie—who has just been rejected by Henry because she refuses to bowl in a topless tournament that he has been pressured into promoting by the Mob—runs hysterically down a lane, trips, and falls headfirst into the automatic ball-return mechanism. She is instantly decapitated. Fade to black.

I sincerely apologize for the previous paragraph, but *The Other Boleyn Girl* annoyed me. A lot.

If you're hooked on Eric Bana, Natalie Portman, or Scarlett Johansson, I suppose that you will want to see *The Other Boleyn Girl* no matter what. But if you enjoy believable and engaging historical dramas, by the end of this you will be cheering for the executioner.

The Queen

(2006)

The Queen is directed by Stephen Frears, who previously directed *Mrs. Henderson Presents*, an amusing comedy that featured
another queenly actress, Dame Judi Dench. Helen Mirren—a
Dame who is also quite good at portraying royalty—had great
success portraying Queen Charlotte in 1994 in *The Madness of
King George*, earning an Oscar nomination for Best Supporting
Actress. Not only is Mirren an exceptional actress who has been
nominated many times for her work on both stage and screen, but
she is also an outspoken, feisty, and eminently quotable actress.
Discussing her profession, Mirren once said, "All you have to do
is to look like crap on film and everyone thinks you're a brilliant
actress. Actually, all you've done is look like crap."

Portraying Elizabeth II in *The Queen*, Mirren does not look
like crap, although she does look a bit frumpy. But the really exciting news is this: if you've always wanted to see the Queen in her
jammies and night gown, here's your chance! We also get to see
Prince Philip (excellently portrayed by James Cromwell) in his
jammies, which is rather comical. We also get to see Tony Blair in
his pyjamas. The movie is practically a pyjama party.

Here's an idea for those who think we need a new political
party in Canada: someone should found the Pyjama Party. I'd
vote for it. Their slogan could be: don't panic, let's sleep on it. The
Brits may have a reputation for being uptight, but their filmmakers are not afraid of showing British politicians in their pjs. In this
country, political leadership races would be over in five minutes if
the candidates showed up for the first debate in their pyjamas. We
would immediately know who to vote for.

The Queen explores and speculates about the difficult days that followed the sudden death of Princess Diana. You will recall that the fatal accident happened early in the morning in Paris, so the royal family as well as the then newly elected Prime Minister, Tony Blair, were literally yanked out of bed and informed in the middle of the night, which explains the predominance of pyjamas in the early going. This film does not have much of a special-effects budget, so the most spectacular special effect is seeing the whole darned royal family in their pjs. Wow.

The Queen presents us with an intelligent and entertaining look behind the closed doors of Buckingham Palace and 10 Downing Street during the crisis, when Britain was mourning for Diana, and when the much-loved and dynamic Tony Blair seemed to have his finger on the populist pulse of Britain. When Diana died, the royal family in general and the Queen in particular seemed completely at sea about how to react to the overwhelming, if not almost insane, public outpouring of grief that washed over the country after her death.

"Insane" is perhaps a harsh word. I don't mean to say that anyone who was saddened by her death is a nut—there was enormous popular sympathy toward her after her perceived mistreatment by the royal family. In the popular mind at least, it was believed that old Charlie had treated her as little more than a royal dish rag. Her death was also seen by some as an opportunity to question the whole idea of a monarchy. Peter Morgan's script makes a very fine point: tragedy always serves someone. There always seems to be someone to profit from any kind of misery, and here the point is made that Diana's death was an opportunity seized upon by Tony Blair's spin doctors and speech writers to have him play to the public mood like a violin virtuoso. The script explores the genesis of Blair's now famous speech, when he coined the phrase "The People's Princess." Blair had recently won a landslide victory, but he wanted to solidify his popularity even more, and his spin experts sold him as the caring, modern face of Britain, in opposition (or at least in contrast) to the icy and uncaring royal family.

When *The Queen* had its premiere at the Venice Film Festival, Helen Mirren received a five-minute standing ovation at the end of the screening. The entire cast is first-rate, but Mirren completely steals the show. It is fairly easy to caricature the Queen—Monty Python used to do it brilliantly—but to portray her in a believable way, given her total lack of emotionalism, is a real challenge. The portrait that emerges is of a person who had a role thrust upon her at an early age—just a young girl and totally unprepared—and who devoted herself to her office even to the exclusion of relationships. Mirren's portrayal of a person who seems almost incapable of basic human warmth and affection is vivid. Ironically, we want to like her, to feel sorry for her even, but she is such a hard case that we just can't connect.

The Queen certainly should not be taken as cinéma-vérité, but the film generates enough docudrama punch to make the audience feel that it certainly might have all happened this way—with archival footage, news reports, and television footage of Diana's funeral put to excellent use. All of this authentic visual material serves to give the film a gritty feel. Diana's death and its aftermath was one of the most heavily mediated news events in the history of the world, and because the footage we are seeing is real, the sense of reality bleeds into the staged dramatic scenes, successfully blurring the line between fact and speculation. *The Queen* focuses on the clash between Tony Blair and Elizabeth, but it also raises questions about the role of media in a world obsessed with celebrity, where the art of governing has been finely focused to ensure that form triumphs over content.

Religulous

(2008)

Let's face it, we all believe in things that are unproven or based in superstition.

I'm a baseball fan. There are more superstitious beliefs rampant in baseball than in any other sport. During the American League Championship Series in 2004, at one point my wife, my son, and I were sitting in the living room watching game four—sitting there with our Red Sox caps turned inside out on our heads. Did we really believe that by doing this, we were going to help the Sox stage a comeback? How does wearing your cap inside out affect the outcome of a game? Does it modify the earth's magnetic field, sending positive waves to the boys in Boston? And if we didn't think it might make a difference, why did we do it? Because we wanted to look silly?

It was a question of faith.

Do you know that the official DVD of the Red Sox 2004 Championship season (yes they went on to win; how could they lose with so many of their fans wearing their caps inside out?) is called *Faith Rewarded*? You can mock faith as Bill Maher does in *Religulous*, you can call it superstition till you're blue in the face; but if someone really believes, you're wasting your breath. And people—most people anyway—seem to need to believe in something. It seems to me that the problem occurs when diversity of belief (or lack of belief, atheism) is perceived as a threat. The problem has never been religious belief; the problem has always been religious intolerance.

— — —

Bill Maher grew up in New Jersey. Although his mother was Jewish, he was raised in the Catholic faith. He says that this gave him a particular perspective on religion—as a Catholic he went to confession, but being part Jewish, he always brought along his lawyer. Ha ha.

Religulous sends us on a journey of discovery as Maher visits Jerusalem, the American heartland, the Vatican—which he gets thrown out of—and a religious theme park in Florida called The Holy Land Experience. Mr. Maher spends his onscreen time talking to members and representatives of various religions, all the while challenging—even openly mocking—their beliefs.

Politically incorrect? You bet.

But many scenes are quite funny. In a recent interview, director Larry Charles stressed the film's mission to "reach beyond the converted, to people who might not ordinarily choose [to see] this movie—people who are moderately religious or even very religious but who have a sense of humour, and realize there's a certain absurdity to some of this."

Charles talks about humour, but when it comes to religion, one man's joke is another man's crucifixion. The sole purpose of this movie is to allow Bill Maher to confront believers of all religions—including Jews, Christians, and Muslims—to essentially tell them that their beliefs are nothing more than a load of superstitious nonsense. Maher is a funny guy, and he hits more than he misses, but after a while you may feel as I did: that the joke wears pretty thin pretty quickly. Some of the humour is sophomoric and the movie cheats a bit by adding onscreen comments and images that support Maher while mocking whoever he's talking to.

It seems a bit like shooting fish in a barrel to mock someone who takes the Old Testament literally. When Maher speaks with American Senator Mark Pryor from Arkansas, who tells him that he believes in creationism, Maher goes all wide-eyed and goofy, "you mean you believe in talking snakes?" To which Pryor answers, "well, you don't have to pass an IQ test to get into the Senate."

Amen to that.

There is a fine moment in *Religulous* when a Vatican scholar states flatly that there is no science in the Old Testament; he says, "these are myths than man used to explain things before we had people like Galileo and the beginnings of scientific thought." No surprises there.

It would be a mistake to accuse Maher of being motivated simply by nastiness. He rightly points out that many of the founding fathers of the United States, Thomas Jefferson for example, were not only disdainful of religion, but also acutely aware of the wisdom of separating church and state. Jefferson once said that "the clergy has converted the simple teachings of Jesus into an engine for enslaving mankind." Maher makes the rather obvious point that if you mix religious fervour, emotionalism, and fundamentalism with political ambition and with weapons of mass destruction, the human race is in dire straits.

To be fair, Maher takes aim at all religions, and he is a gutsy social critic. I don't agree with everything he says, however. It seems to me that it is not religion itself that is at fault; many people accept their religion as a personal thing and are not intolerant toward other beliefs. But there are many who put words into God's mouth, and claim that they know the will of God, thereby giving themselves carte blanche when it comes to any kind of action. There are some scenes in *Religulous* of protesters carrying signs that read God Hates Homosexuals. Maher confronts someone about this, telling him "Jesus never said anything about homosexuality. He did however make a lot of statements about the evils of money and of greed, yet you don't see the religious right carrying signs reading God Hates Millionaires or God Hates Wall Street," (although that may be coming soon). His point is a good one: why is there such a homophobic streak running through Christian fundamentalism?

Maher is a natural doo-doo disturber, and I have always found people like this interesting. *Religulous* is one of those rare movies that have the potential to offend people across the board, but I encourage you, dear reader (no matter your beliefs or non-beliefs), to see it. I applaud any movie that questions dogma. Don't be afraid, it's only a movie.

Anyway, all religions believe things that are pretty strange. For example, did you know that Mormons believe that the Garden of Eden was in Missouri? Well, why not? Missouri is rather pretty. If they believed it was in Buffalo, now that would be weird. I was raised as a Catholic and the virgin birth is something that Maher harps on a lot as being downright ridiculous, but two thousand years later we have in vitro fertilization, which you could argue is a virgin birth of sorts. So who knows? *Chariots of the Gods* may be starting to make sense.

Road to Nowhere

(2010)

Q: What exactly is a cult director?
A: That's a tough one.

Are we talking about a director whose films have limited (or zero) commercial success, yet have received a certain level of critical praise? Or a director who, despite a relative lack of commercial success, manages to inspire great enthusiasm—if not fanaticism—in his audience? Or possibly a director who has had commercial success, but is also known for making quirky, low-budget films that are warmly received by cult moviegoers? Or directors who have made films that are so out-to-lunch, or spectacularly inept, that they have garnered the undying love of midnight movie audiences? Or all of the above?

The preceding definitions could apply to a diverse crop of directors—what is the term for a group of directors anyway? Inflated egos often being on parade, perhaps they should be called a pride of directors. David Lynch, Francis Ford Coppola, Werner Herzog, Robert Altman, Roger Corman, Ed Wood, and Pedro Almodovar; any list of so-called cult directors would be incredibly eclectic. And as previously mentioned, many of these directors have had spectacular commercial success, but they have also travelled to the very brink of commercial filmmaking, and in some cases gone right over the edge in their desire to explore strange new worlds. Who is the real Francis Ford Coppola: the director of *The Godfather* or the director of *Rumble Fish*? Which Lynch directed *Eraserhead* and which directed *The Straight Story*?

There is no such ambiguity when discussing the films of American director Monte Hellman. The peculiar, low-budget films he has concocted over the years have titles like *Back Door to Hell* (1964), *The Shooting* (1966), *Two-Lane Blacktop* (1971), and *Iguana* (1988). He is not a prolific director. *Road to Nowhere* is his first film in twenty years.

Some critics consider *The Shooting* to be the first Acid Western. If spaghetti Westerns give you indigestion, you will definitely want to avoid Acid Westerns. The term dates from the nineties when film critic Jonathan Rosenbaum used it to describe the Jim Jarmusch film *Dead Man* starring Johnny Depp. I reviewed *Dead Man* for CBC Radio way back in 1995.

I do not use the word "hate" lightly, but I can say without any hesitation that I hated *Dead Man*. I called it "an incredibly slow and pointless filmic exercise . . . a kind of avant-garde, artsy, black-and-white Western which I found almost impossible to enjoy in any way."

Let's keep those words in mind as we go down the road to nowhere.

Monte Hellman turned eighty in 2012. He learned his craft in the fifties and sixties under the tutelage of the "King of the B-Movies," Roger Corman. In 1966 Hellman was the editor on Corman's legendary biker exploitation film, *The Wild Angels*. Corman gave Jack Nicholson his first roles and Nicholson also starred in Hellman's two Acid Westerns, *Ride in the Whirlwind* and *The Shooting*. Both were made for about $70,000 and shot within a few weeks of each other in 1965.

According to aficionados, the Acid Western borrows heavily from the counterculture values of the sixties and portrays society as a nightmarish dystopia. A critic more eloquent than me — yes there are a few, not many, but a few — described *The Shooting* as "savage frontier poetry served up to justify its hallucinated agenda." Some of you will recognize that this is exactly the kind of gobbledygook that gets thrown around when critics, who are generally pretty normal people, are confronted with cinematic works so obtuse and opaque that they make the critic's brain feel as if it has been placed in a Cuisinart set on liquefy.

Another important point—or gross generalization, you decide—about cult films is that they originally bombed at the box office but over the years, with the advent of repertory cinemas and (let's face it) cheap recreational drugs, these films have attained a kind of undead status. They live between dusk and dawn at midnight screenings filled with demi-monde film buffs, ageing hipsters, and flickering shadow people.

Which brings us to *Road to Nowhere*.

The first thing I would like to say is that Monte Hellman is not a hack with a camera. He is a director who learned his craft, paid his dues, and made artistic choices. Like the young filmmakers in *Road to Nowhere*, he intentionally if not ferociously shuns the commercial path. *Road to Nowhere* is a movie within a movie about a young writer-director making a film concerning a real-life double suicide involving a rich state official and his young girlfriend. Amusingly, when casting the film, the director rejects the idea of using Leonardo DiCaprio in the lead and also rejects Scarlett Johansson for the female lead even though, incredibly, her agent says she will work for scale. The script is filled with references like these to the inner workings of the movie business, and I found these inside jokes to be easily the most amusing bits of the movie. And in that sense, *Road to Nowhere* is very roughly cut from the same cloth (or, on a smaller budget, the same burlap sack) as *The Player*, and there is even a direct reference to Robert Altman—a director who very successfully walked the tightrope between commercialism and cultish offerings. At one point, grappling with his script, the screenwriter wonders aloud "how would Altman do this?" That being said, to compare Monte Hellman's films to anyone else is to advance on very thin ice, yet I couldn't help but be reminded of David Lynch's *Mulholland Drive*, another confusing movie about the process of making movies. And like *Road to Nowhere*, *Mulholland Drive* also features a female lead who may or may not be who we think she is—even she doesn't seem quite sure. But as obscure as *Mulholland Drive* was in spots, *Road to Nowhere* ups the narrative ante considerably by offering not only a movie about someone making a movie, but about someone making a movie *about* making a movie.

Wheee!

By the way, I watched *Road to Nowhere* on DVD, so I had the luxury of backing up and watching scenes over again. It didn't help.

Hellman's films are inhabited by characters consumed by the urge to forge ahead, whether or not there is actually anywhere to go. The young filmmakers in *Road to Nowhere* bear some resemblance to the coyote in the Chuck Jones Roadrunner cartoons—figuratively speaking, of course. As absurd as this comparison might seem on the surface, I think that both Hellman and Jones share, to a lighter or darker degree, a vision of American life as an ultimately absurd, unwinnable carnival game; their frantic characters are aiming for a bit of heaven, but they are ultimately trapped on a wild and bumpy rollercoaster ride to oblivion.

Road to Nowhere begins with a shot of a DVD being loaded into a laptop. The title of the DVD is *Road to Nowhere*. Bravo, Mr. Hellman! Before we have even settled into the batter's box, the director has us flailing away at knuckleballs. Is *Road to Nowhere* the movie we are watching? Or are we watching the movie in the DVD player, or both, or neither?

A young director named Mitchell Haven—note the same initials as our real director, Monte Hellman—is casting a movie called *Road to Nowhere*. He has, with great difficulty, persuaded an actress named Laurel Graham to portray the victim of a sensational double suicide case. The real case has remained open for years because both the insurance company, as well as an investigative blogger named Nathalie, believe that the deaths may actually have been faked as an insurance scam. Nathalie suspects that the alleged victims are alive and well, possibly in Italy. To further confuse matters, the person watching the DVD on the laptop is the attractive blonde blogger Nathalie, and she is watching the DVD in the company of the director.

Are you still with me, Major Tom?

Now things get really interesting. The actress cast in the role of the suicide victim looks remarkably like the dead woman—could she actually be the dead woman, and wouldn't this explain why she was extremely reluctant to accept the role? But then why would she even consider for a second playing her supposedly dead self?

But it all gets even thicker. Her lover was supposed to have died after he crashed his plane into a lake, but he is also a character in the movie within a movie, and he appears to be alive and living in Rome.

It was at this point that I paused the DVD and reached for the Gaviscon (blatant product placement). I don't mind having a character appearing in a movie within a movie—Naomi Watts as Diane Selwyn does this in *Mulholland Drive*—but I get a little fidgety when I don't know which movie the character is in. It is a tribute to the director's considerable editing skills that any of this can hold together as well as it does, considering that both movies run the audience around in circles for two hours. After the first hour I did not know which movie I was supposed to be watching, and I was feeling woozy. Not only was my heartburn kicking in, but I was also developing what used to be known back in the seventies as an Excedrin headache (more product placement—this movie may be low-budget, but the review is going to be lucrative).

On the plus side, much of the action (for lack of a better term) in *Road to Nowhere* takes place at night and the cinematography is absolutely first-rate; the movie oozes atmosphere. But then so does a punctured weather balloon.[3]

Road to Nowhere is the kind of film that encourages critics, who are often desperate, to flights of excessive verbosity. Not wanting to appear unhip or left behind, the desperate critic will sometimes close his eyes and fling the analytical manure at the swiftly rotating ventilation device with such enthusiasm that the poor moviegoer is left with head spinning like Linda Blair in *The Exorcist*. Allow me now to cut to the chase: this movie makes no

---

3   In nearly twenty years of reviewing films, this is the first time I have ever compared a movie to a weather balloon, punctured or otherwise. I don't really know how this happened, it just did. I'll try not to do it again.

sense. Period. It is a stylish, often engaging, but mostly infuriating piece of postmodern navel gazing. I trust that the filmmaker knew what he was doing—I believe this, I truly do—but I can assure him that I, as a spectator, had not the faintest idea. I felt a bit like Cary Grant in *North by Northwest*, abandoned at a bus stop in the middle of nowhere without even a crop-dusting plane to entertain me.

Shark Night 3D

(2011)

You have to be suspicious of a summer popcorn horror movie that gets released in September. Summer movies are a lot like driftwood: the really nice pieces tend to float in early with the tide and are quickly picked up. By the time the tide starts going out, there isn't much left to pick over. If a movie aimed at a teenage audience has been held back until this late in the season, it may not have been worth releasing in the first place. At the very least, the producers certainly didn't believe that it could compete with the A-list summer fare.

Over thirty-five years after the ground-breaking release of *Jaws*, you would think that shark movies would be passé. Yet every year, when I go to Maine for my summer vacation, it's Shark Week on the Discovery Channel. I am told that some people plan their summer around this television event, and throw Shark Week pool parties and all kinds of nutty events. It is even whispered, and this is the incredibly inane premise of *Shark Night 3D*, that some hardcore shark junkies will pay big bucks to see reality footage of shark attacks—the real sicko stuff that your run-of-the-mill cable provider just won't provide.

Shark Night 3D is directed, or at least poked at, by David R. Ellis. Ellis had a long and successful career as a first-rate stuntman before he tried his hand at directing. He may have been a great stuntman, but when it comes to directing, he tends to fall flat on his face. His hit parade includes *Final Destination 2* (which got my vote for silliest title that year; I mean, if the first one was the final destination, there's nowhere left to go), *Snakes on a Plane*, *Cellular* (which featured some of Kim Basinger's best screaming ever), and *Asylum* (a bloody mess of a movie). I am surprised that there have so far been no sequels to *Snakes on a Plane*; this seemed to me a franchise that had huge potential: *Snakes on a Bus, Snakes in the Jacuzzi, Snakes in the Vacuum Cleaner*, and of course, one of the all-time great sexploitation concepts, *Snakes in the Locker Room*. It is rumoured that Ellis' next project is something called *Zombie Blondes*—from the title alone I'll venture that this could be the one he'll be remembered for. When it comes to crummy movies, David R. Ellis is a seasoned vet, which by the way is apparently also a favourite snack food of carnivorous zoo animals.

Shark Night 3D will stand the test of time—it will be the reference for years to come when we talk about shark movies, right down there with *Deep Blue Sea* (remember that one?). It featured Samuel L. Jackson uttering the immortal line, "these sharks are thinking . . . hard and clear!" and "that's the answer to the riddle. Because that's what an eight-thousand pound mako thinks about. About freedom. About the deep blue sea." Well, I have no idea what eight-thousand pound mako sharks think about (they actually don't exist; the maximum weight for a mako is fifteen hundred pounds), but I do know that the writers of *Deep Blue Sea* were not thinking hard and clear when they concocted this nonsense. The writers of *Shark Night 3D*, Will Hayes and Jesse Studenberg, do not fare any better. By the way, Hayes is the writer behind the animated series *Assy McGee*, so we just knew that this was going to be a quality script.

Plot time: Seven mostly obnoxious and unlikeable college kids go off to a lake cottage for the weekend. The lake is in Louisiana, and it turns out to be one of those darned lakes that have freshwater sharks in them. For about the first twenty minutes, before the first shark appears, I thought I was watching an extended Budweiser commercial, but with more risqué situations. Then one of the boys, a football star, gets an arm torn off while waterskiing. Incredibly, he doesn't bleed to death because another young man, a med student, applies a tourniquet. Never mind that he would have bled to death ten minutes earlier—suspend your disbelief. Our now one-armed football star will later actually get up out of bed clutching a spear (!) in his hand and wade out into the lake to confront the shark that ate his girlfriend.

Note to the director: *The Shark That Ate His Girlfriend* sounds like a cool title for a sequel.

This group of students includes two characters who will obviously survive in the end — all of the other boys and girls are wearing those very trendy brand clothes and tiny bikinis that expendable crew members always wear in these movies. The tiny bikinis are put to good use in the underwater 3D scenes as the camera focuses in on the female posteriors. There are lots of air bubbles in this movie also, and I think that we can all agree that you haven't truly experienced the full power of 3D until you have been inundated with air bubbles floating around bikini bottoms. I can't wait to see this in IMAX.

After the football jock got chomped I was cheering for the sharks. It is a multiracial group — most of the major shark food groups are represented — as the football star is Black, his girlfriend is Hispanic, and the other kids are white. So the sharks get to choose between soul food, spicy Latino, and white turkey meat.

But I haven't even mentioned the creepy, hillbilly locals. The head hillbilly used to be the heroine's boyfriend until she announced three years before that she was going off to college. Upset at her decision, he tried to drown her. In retaliation, she ran a motorboat propeller over his face. He still holds a grudge; go figure. When she is placed in a shark cage by this yahoo, she pleads with him, saying, "that was three years ago; can't you just let it go?"

Apparently not.

Anyway, the hillbillies may or may not be releasing these sharks into the lake in order to film fatal shark attacks. They then sell the gruesome video footage on the Internet to the assorted weirdos, wackos, and yoyos who find the Discovery Channel's Shark Week too wimpy.

In fairness — and I'm nothing if not fair-minded — the cast of young unknowns does quite well under the circumstances (i.e., a crummy script seasoned with ridiculous dialogue). And the sharks turn in some pretty strong performances also. The 3D effects are insipid. Part *Jaws*, part Budweiser Super Bowl commercial, and part *Deliverance*, *Shark Night 3D* is all rip off. It is indeed a serious contender for Stinker of the Year. That being said, I did find myself laughing in a few places. If the writers had opted for a satirical approach then perhaps this could have been saved, but as it is, it takes itself seriously, which is a fatal mistake. And speaking of fatal, while doing some research on the Internet, I actually found a forum that discusses the question of how long it would take to bleed to death if you had your arm cut off. One of the participants in the forum concluded that he didn't know, but thought "if you had your head cut off, it would be pretty quick." No argument there. However, I don't think that you die from loss of blood if your head is cut off; I think that you die because, hey, your head's cut off. Watching *Shark Night 3D* will provide you with an experience not unlike having your head cut off.

Slither

(2006)

Let me set the scene. A meteor from the deepest recesses of space is hurtling toward earth. The meteorite lands in the woods and, behaving like your typical sci-fi movie meteorite, it breaks open and starts to glow and ooze some stuff that looks suspiciously like melted gummy bears. The small town of Wheelsy is about to be invaded by slithering red slugs that look a lot like spicy sausage.

Note to young aspiring sci-fi movie directors: You don't need a lot of money for special effects; all you need is several bags of gummy bears that you microwave at fifty percent power for about five minutes. You then mix some fluorescent paint into the glop, and presto! Alien goo.

So, the alien meteorite is filled with the equivalent of gummy goo. Not bad for a start, but it gets better. Now, in this little town there is a beautiful young high school biology teacher named Starla (Elizabeth Banks—Laura Bush in *W.*). She is married to Grant (Michael Rooker—*The Walking Dead*), an older fella who is the richest man in the county. Grant looks like an ex-marine drill sergeant. By the way, his family name is Grant, so I guess his parents either weren't too bright or they had a nasty sense of humour, because his name is Grant Grant. Starla doesn't really love him—we know this because when Grant tries to get romantic, she tells him that she's not in the mood. He gets upset and storms out of the house, heading for the local karaoke bar to get drunk (which is an excellent idea because if you've heard most people warbling in karaoke bars, you know that alcohol deadens your critical faculties and your hearing). While in the bar, Grant meets a young woman named Brenda and they wind up out in the woods, and guess what? Grant spots the meteorite and they both follow a slimy trail into the woods. They find this disgusting-looking blob that shoots a needle-like thing right at Grant's chest, and then this slimy blob wriggles its way into Grant's chest while he writhes around in pain. Think of the infamous chest-bursting scene in *Alien*, but in reverse. There are scenes in *Slither* that make *Alien* look like *My Dinner with André*.

The next morning Grant is behaving, as they say around Wheelsy, "mighty peculiar," although he does become very romantic with Starla. Yuck. He also unfortunately develops a constant craving for meat. Raw meat. He buys twenty steaks from the butcher, and begins to feed on any small animals he can get his hands on—neighbourhood dogs are now on the menu. His diet consists mainly of raw meat and raccoons. Yum.

Grant also padlocks the basement, which arouses some suspicions in Starla, but this being a movie, she lets it go. Never mind how incredible this alien invasion stuff is; my incredulity was pushed to the limit when Grant padlocked the basement door and Starla didn't do what every wife in the observable universe would do, namely, call the fire department and have them break it down.

Guys, try padlocking the basement and see how your wife reacts.

But what *is* Grant doing down there? Did he just set up a pool table, or is it much, much worse? Actually, Grant has set up a little den in the basement where he keeps his raw meat and dead animals. It's pretty cozy. You see, Grant is evolving into a really slimy squid-like creature that is going to take over the world unless the brave young chief of police named Bill (Nathan Fillion)—who has been carrying a torch for Starla since high school—can stop him.

Slither is actually entertaining in a weird and thoroughly revolting way. The characters are rather endearing—I was certainly cheering for them. As written and directed by James Gunn, the movie is—depending on your point of view—either extremely derivative of every sci-fi and horror film ever made, or a very good parody of the genre. Gunn made his first movie, on video, at the age of twelve. It was a comedy-splatter film that featured his brothers being disembowelled by zombies. He hasn't really moved on since then. A few years ago, he wrote the screenplay for *Scooby-Doo 2*, which I haven't seen but which is probably a lot more frightening than *Slither*, although for completely different reasons. Given the choice between Scooby-Doo and slithering slugs, I'll take the slugs.

After seeing *Slither*, I went home and jotted down all of the movies that *Slither* borrows from. I came up with *Night of the Living Dead* for zombies and cannibalism—I haven't yet mentioned that when someone gets infected in *Slither*, they turn into a zombie. Other influences are *The Hidden*, which has slimy, tentacle-like things popping out of people; *Alien*, also for slimy things that pop out of people and for the idea of the human body as host or womb for alien critters; and *The Blob*, for meteorites that crack open to reveal slimy, gooey stuff that comes at you. There is also *The Exorcist*, for projectile vomiting of green liquid (in this case, it's some kind of green acid that is vomited by the zombified townsfolk); *The Thing*, for disgusting, rubbery special effects, and again for the idea of human as host; and *Monthy Python's The Meaning of Life* (seriously), for people exploding after eating way too much. Poor Brenda, who has been turned into a host for thousands of these slug creatures, eventually explodes and releases the little varmints.

Once these little varmints have been released, they slither along smartly until they find a human—preferably a teenage girl in a bathtub—and then one slips into the tub.

Whoopee!

This is far more frightening and not nearly as funny as the scene in *The Big Lebowski* where three nihilists drop an attack marmot into the Dude's tub—one of the great scenes in film history, certainly. Anyway, this slug thing tries to get into her mouth, but our tough teenager manages to remove it. The rest of her family isn't so lucky. They are turned into flesh-eating zombies, and their diction goes to hell—notice that when people turn into zombies in the movies, they invariably sound like they've got hot potatoes in their mouths, or in this case, a hot slug.

When citing influences earlier, I forgot to mention a great baseball movie, *Bull Durham*. No, this isn't a typo. You may recall that in *Bull Durham*, Kevin Costner' s character, Crash Davis, is always calling Nook Laloosh (Tim Robbins) "meat," which is a way to bring Nook's big ego down to earth. In *Slither*, when the zombies spot someone who is a potential snack, they say, "meat . . . meat . . ." This is occasionally nerve wracking but often quite funny, albeit in a twisted, I wouldn't want to admit to my therapist that I found that funny, kind of way. The style of black humour that permeates *Slither* evokes two better movies: *Tremors*, which was very entertaining, and *Shaun of the Dead*, a brilliant parody of zombie movies, which had a lot of dry British wit. *Slither* isn't so much tongue-in-cheek as slug-in-mouth, but it's still pretty funny in spots, as when poor two-thousand-pound Brenda, who is full of about-to-be-born alien slugs, looks at the sheriff and delivers the understatement of the century: "There's something wrong with me." Or when Starla confronts her former husband, Grant, who has turned into a gigantic squid-like creature with tentacles; as she's trying to get close enough to stick a knife in him, she's trying to convince him that she still loves him. She looks at his writhing mass and says, "It's going to take me some time to adjust." You bet.

If you're a guy and you love horror movies (B movies in particular), and if you are looking for a movie that will completely gross out your wife/girlfriend, you've hit the jackpot with *Slither*. This is a movie that goes over the top, and then keeps right on going.

I had a brilliant idea for a marketing gimmick. In the old days of gimmick horror movies, the theatres would have silly promotions like "bloodcorn," which was just popcorn with red food dye on it, but it looked really disgusting. If the theatres wanted to get creative with *Slither*, instead of hot dogs they could advertise "slug dogs"—just make the wiener a little lumpier, and you might have a real winner.

Fans of slimy, bodily fluid-filled plots will want to check out two classics of the genre: David Cronenberg's *Shivers*, one of the most repulsive films of all time, and David Lynch's *Eraserhead*, which is not only revolting, but also pretty much indescribable.

Bon appétit.

Straw Dogs

(2011)

The director of this remake, Rod Lurie, used to be a movie critic. He is not the first movie critic to reinvent himself as a director—François Truffaut comes to mind as someone who had spectacular success taking the plunge—but Lurie is not Truffaut, and neither is he Sam Peckinpah, who directed the original version of *Straw Dogs* in 1971. He is Rod Lurie. Don't misunderstand me, there is absolutely nothing wrong with being Rod Lurie—at least not that I know of—but his work will inevitably be compared to Peckinpah's original, a film that was highly controversial at the time of its release, and which still packs a wallop today.

After watching the new version of *Straw Dogs*, I was reminded of a quote by the American writer Edward Dahlberg who said, "It takes a long time to understand nothing."

In the case of this remake, I can tell you, unequivocally, that it takes exactly one hundred and ten minutes. *Straw Dogs* the remake is really interesting but for all the wrong reasons. You may remember that in the original a young American mathematician (Dustin Hoffman), disgusted with the growing violence in America, moves with his British-born wife to Cornwall in England. Once there he is unable to fit in with the locals, and his generally wussy behaviour places him squarely in the sights of the locals until he and his wife are trapped in an escalating nightmare of menace and violence as all kinds of terrible things start to happen, including the yokels hanging their cat.

Note: The Oxford Canadian Dictionary of Current English defines "wussy" as "feeble or cowardly behaviour."

But even a wuss has a breaking point, and after his wife is raped, Hoffman's character goes ballistic. After the drunken locals kill the magistrate and attack his house, our mathematician discards his slide rule and imagines creative uses for a bear trap and boiling whiskey—much nastiness ensues. The movie becomes a festival of Peckinpahnian carnage, and whatever light veneer of civilization the character had at the beginning is peeled away in long bloody strips.

With the exception of John Schlesinger's *Midnight Cowboy* released two years before, no mainstream Hollywood movie had ever depicted this level of violence or explicit sexual situations. Many accused Peckinpah of glorifying violence and pandering to the audience's baser instincts, but *Straw Dogs* raised some disturbing and still timely questions about morality and the hypocrisy of civilization. We have to remember that in 1971, the USA was advertising itself—as it does today—as a moral, God-fearing society, even as it was dropping napalm on Vietnamese civilians. Forty years later, if we substitute Iraq for Vietnam, we see that *plus ça change, plus c'est la même chose.*

This new version tries to resonate politically by pointing the finger at what the director seems to feel are the root causes of violence in America. The hero represents West Coast liberalism, and the bad guys are almost certainly Republican voters (i.e., they love cars and guns, and football and guns, and trucks and guns). And we also get the expected mix of religious fervour, twisted to fit the prevailing political ideology. These folks are convinced that if Jesus came back down to earth today, he'd probably crack open a few beers with us and do some shootin' . . . yes sir, hyuh-hyuh!"[4]

— — —

Plot: Hollywood screenwriter David Sumner (James Marsden) and his attractive starlet wife, Amy (Kate Bosworth), are driving down the road in his 1967 Jaguar while singing along to the classic Monkees hit "Going Down." They pull into the town of Blackwater, Mississippi, and park in front of Blackie's, the local redneck watering hole.

Perfect, I thought. How fitting that the Monkees song is about suicide. The last thing you want to do is park an ostentatious

---

4   Hillbilly-type laugh

sports car in front of a redneck bar while the radio is blaring the Monkees, when the place is filled with a lot of big, ugly-looking locals who are already half-drunk at noon and listening to Lynyrd Skynyrd.

This is Amy's hometown, and she and David have decided to move into her daddy's house so that David can get some peace and quiet while he is writing a screenplay about the battle of Stalingrad (!).

Time for a little role playing. You are David. You decide that you and your wife, Amy, are going to have lunch in the neighbourhood diner; you settle down in a booth and order some local BBQ. Soon a big, muscular guy walks over to your table and says hello to your wife, who he calls "Amycakes." The guy is Charlie, Amy's ex, the former high school football star turned professional hillbilly-yahoo-troublemaker (Amy was head cheerleader in high school). He looks like he eats screenwriters for breakfast, and probably washes them down with a few Budweisers. Now, you mention that the roof of Amy's daddy's barn needs repairs. Charlie says that he can supply a team to do the job. How do you respond?

A) You tell Charlie that you are receiving tenders for the work, but that he will certainly be considered

B) You decide, right then and there, to heck with the barn because there is absolutely no way that Charlie and his buddies are getting within five hundred yards of your house, or

C) You smile enthusiastically like a total moron and announce right then and there that heck, Charlie, you're an old flame of Amy's and "as far as I'm concerned, the job is yours; when can you start?"

If you answered "C" as our hero does, don't you think that you deserve everything that's coming to you?

Let's try another one. Having hired the yahoos to repair your barn, you are rudely awakened at some ungodly hour by the sound of Charlie and the boys firing up a buzz saw. Do you:

A) Get dressed, put on some shoes, and climb up the ladder to the barn roof to tell Charlie, in no uncertain terms, that you don't want them to start before nine in the morning;

B) Go outside while still in your jammies and slippers—those comfy ones with the fuzzy synthetic fur—climb up the ladder and say meekly, "isn't it a little early guys?" or

C) Get dressed, call the guys down from the roof and tell them that if they want to have this job, they are going to have to play by your rules. "It's my money, it's my rules, and I don't want to see you guys on the roof before nine in the morning."

If you answered "B," you can probably expect that very soon, Charlie and his buddies are going to stuff your fuzzy slippers up your nose, or worse.

I haven't even described David and Amy's reaction to finding their cat strangled in the closet, but the word that comes to mind is "wussy," as in, "they had a wussy reaction."

The nastiest of the locals is Tom, the retired high school football coach, portrayed by James Woods. Tom is a mean, manipulative, and vicious drunk. Woods gives a fine performance here, and I couldn't wait for him to get boiling oil thrown at him, or to get his feet blown off with a shotgun.

Sorry; bit of a spoiler there.

Actually, it isn't really possible to spoil this movie in the traditional sense because everything that happens is totally inevitable and predictable. For example, when I spotted a big old bear trap on display in the living room, I immediately wondered how long it would take before someone got their head stuck in it. The answer, by the way, is ninety-seven minutes. Just to illustrate how subtle this movie is: when David (insanely) agrees to go hunting with Charlie and the boys, he is handed an orange jacket to wear, and (amazingly) there is no target on David's jacket. That's as subtle as it gets.

When it comes to movie violence and what audiences found upsetting and objectionable back in 1971, we have come a very long way indeed. But is it progress? Forty years ago, the violence in this remake of *Straw Dogs* would have guaranteed an X rating. That being said, in comparison to some of the video games the kids are playing these days, *Straw Dogs* is pretty tame.

But for all of its violence and sleaze, *Straw Dogs* is amazingly dull. For movie violence to really disturb an audience, the movie has to begin by making the viewer care about the characters.

I didn't like anybody in this movie. Well, okay, maybe I did feel bad about the cat. Oh, and the sheriff. Incredibly, this redneck town full of drunken yahoos has a Black sheriff. We are told that he is an Iraqi war hero. As soon as I saw him I thought, poor guy; he should have stayed in Iraq, at least he would have had a fighting chance. James Woods fanatics might get some enjoyment from watching this, but everyone else is doomed. As a rental, I suggest skipping over all the scenes that don't feature Woods, and you will have a pretty good twenty-minute movie.

Synecdoche, New York

(2008)

Synecdoche is pronounced "sin-eck-duh-key." A synecdoche is a figure of speech in which a part is used to represent the whole, or the whole for a part. For example, "the Red Sox are glad to have another *arm* in the bullpen," or "*Toronto* hasn't won the Stanley Cup since Ron Tugnutt was born."

I don't mean to suggest by that last example that the sad state of the Leafs is in any way related to the birth of Mr. Tugnutt.

Synecdoche is also a terrible title for a movie. Any word that no one knows how to pronounce is a bad title for a movie. If no one can pronounce it, it can't possibly be a hit. No one wants to go to the box office and request a ticket for a movie and have the kid at the counter laugh at them, or even worse, correct their pronunciation.

Note to aspiring actors: If you want to be a popular actor, it is very important that people are able to pronounce your name. Case in point: Keir Dullea. He is a fine actor (he portrayed Dave in *2001: A Space Odyssey*) but his career never really took off because no one knew how to pronounce his name. You do not get invited to talk shows if the host doesn't know how to pronounce your name. By the way, his name is apparently pronounced "Care Dullay," but it's a bit late for that—he is in his late seventies. And while we're on the subject, *Quantum of Solace* is also a terrible title for a movie because who in heck knows what that even means?

It seems to me that strong, vibrant writing comes from a very personal point of view. In writing class they always tell you to "write what you know." If you tell a personal story and tell it well and honestly, then you will touch many other lives because even though Joseph Conrad said "we live as we dream—alone," we also have a shared humanity. Yes, even if you're a Leafs fan, you are not alone—you can commiserate with Cubs fans and Detroit Lions fans. Suffering is universal.

Now in the case of the wildly ambitious and overwrought *Synecdoche, New York*, the screenwriter, Charlie Kaufman, has set out to tell the story of everybody and everything: to write the great American movie. And I think that the project was doomed from the first inning because to be able to relate to a story, the audience needs to sink its collective teeth into the particular, the personal. It is only through the particular that the essence of the general experience of life can be distilled.

Synecdoche is incredibly experimental for a Hollywood film. Light years removed from mainstream cinema, it never had the slightest wisp of a chance being a commercial success, although it probably had a much better chance of being successful than David Lynch's *Inland Empire* (see review listed earlier in this book). After all, *Synecdoche* is about an hour shorter than Lynch's opaque opus, and it makes a lot more sense.

Unlike Lynch, who seemed to be making it up as he went along in *Inland Empire*, screenwriter and first-time director Charlie Kaufman has very meticulously constructed *Synecdoche*. The movie is focused, analyzing the life of one character, a theatre director named Caden Cotard. But the script is impossibly ambitious, trying to present something akin to the unified field theory of life as theatre—recognizing every individual as the author of his own tragedy. This is intriguing, but the vision presented is terribly bleak, not to mention hopelessly confusing. Near the end of the film, the narrator tells us that life begins with great expectations but that disappointments and detours dim those hopes while loved ones fall away through the years. This leaves us with the sad realization that none of us is very special after all; rather, "everyone is everyone." The only thing missing is "I am he as you are he as you are me and we are all together."

From his very first screenplay, *Being John Malkovich*, Charlie Kaufman established himself as a unique voice. There is practically no one working in Hollywood who writes these kinds of surrealistic stories. And when he is on his game, as he was spectacularly with *Eternal Sunshine of the Spotless Mind* (2004), the results are wondrous and wildly entertaining. But even Ted Williams struck out occasionally.

No plot synopsis can really hope to explain what is going on in *Synecdoche*, but here goes nothing: A small-time theatre director named Caden Cotard (Philip Seymour Hoffman) is struggling personally and professionally. His wife has left him to pursue her own artistic ambitions in Berlin, and she has taken their young daughter with her. A new relationship with an unstable woman named Hazel (Samantha Morton in one of her now-patented wacky roles) is going nowhere. Unexpectedly Caden receives something called a genius grant, which includes a large sum of money. Eventually, our hero mounts a gigantic play based on his own life that functions on multiple levels as actors are hired to portray his friends and family, and other actors are hired to portray the actors portraying the friends and family (!). If this all sounds confusing, it is. But I could have lived with the confusion if the action (such as it is) hadn't slowed to a deadly crawl in the second hour.

It's important to note that the hero Caden Cotard is a hypochondriac who is seemingly incapable of having fun or seeing life in a positive light. Seymour Hoffman is a great actor and he pulls out all the stops for this role, but in the end, his character is incredibly irritating. I didn't like this person, but more importantly, I didn't care if he was miserable.

And maybe that's the point.

By presenting us with a character who is not remotely likeable, Kaufman is throwing down the dramatic gauntlet — challenging our basic expectations of how the hero of a film is supposed to behave and how he is supposed to endear himself to us. I suppose that by challenging the audience to follow, in minute detail, the story of a man it dislikes, Kaufman hopes that his script will more closely resemble real life; after all, our lives are filled with people we don't particularly like or care about but are still curious about. It is a very risky dramatic gambit, and for my money, it never pays off.

The character's name, Cotard, is interesting. There exists a medical condition, the Cotard delusion or Cotard's syndrome, that is also known as nihilistic or negation delusion. It is a very rare neuropsychiatric disorder in which a person holds a delusional belief that he or she is dead or does not exist. This is significant because *Synecdoche* is preoccupied with nothing less than the very meaning of existence. What is real? What is illusion? Let's not forget also that the term "synecdoche" has Greek roots and means "simultaneous understanding."

I apologize if this is starting to sound like Philosophy in Film 101: Existential motifs and characterizations in the work of Charlie Kaufman.

A quote from Robert Browning comes to mind here: "A man's reach should exceed his grasp, or what's a heaven for?" I applaud Kaufman for reaching so high, but I ultimately could grasp little of what he was trying to say, and the experience of sitting through *Synecdoche* is far from heavenly.

Kaufman's best scripts communicate a surrealistic sense of fun and discovery. In *Synecdoche*, everything gets very bleak, very fast. Despite some powerful performances from Seymour Hoffman and the great Samantha Morton, and despite some terrific cinematography and superb set design, Charlie Kaufman's *Synecdoche* doesn't work. The film takes itself terribly seriously. Instead of the playful and mischievous self-mockery that he served up in *Adaptation* (2002), Kaufman indulges in existential hand-wringing on a monumental scale. Again, perhaps this is Kaufman's point: the character is doomed precisely because he takes himself too seriously, because he is self-obsessed.

I agree with the sentiment, but the method leaves me dazed and confused. *Synecdoche* is an unfocused, frustrating film. On the plus side it marks another tour-de-force performance for Philip Seymour Hoffman, and I applaud any filmmaker who can go out on the edge like this with a big-budget film—lord knows, as a moviegoer, I'm sick of being fed the cinematic equivalent of pureed carrots and peas. Great art is built on taking chances, and

Charlie Kaufman missing the mark is still a lot more interesting than a lesser filmmaker hitting the same easy target over and over again, but *Synecdoche* stretched my patience to the breaking point. It is unfortunate that a story about a man who is hopelessly self-obsessed is presented in a film that I can only qualify as hopelessly self-absorbed. Charlie Kaufman is a brilliant writer, but along the road to *Synecdoche, New York* he seems to have forgotten all about the poor audience sitting out there in the dark, desperate for some entertainment.

True Grit

(2010)

Some of you know that I am a big fan of the Western—that most resilient of Hollywood genres. The Western never really gets old because it has the ability, when written and directed by particularly astute artists, to reinvent itself and to remain relevant, even in this Twitter-crazed, Facebook-fascinated, BlackBerry-addled culture.

Cinematography is vitally important in a Western, not only because the spectacular landscapes and sweeping vistas of the West often serve as backdrop to the story, but also because the cinematography can do much to give a contemporary audience a sense of the period—a time of dance halls illuminated by gaslight and candles, when barrooms were a dark haven from the blazing midday sun, and glistening steam engines brought the promise of prosperity to dusty, one-horse towns. One of the great contemporary cinematographers is Roger Deakins who photographed one of the great Westerns of recent memory, *The Assassination of Jesse James by the Coward Robert Ford*, which is a stunningly beautiful film. Deakins also photographed *Fargo* and *No Country for Old Men* for the Coen brothers, and he is once again behind the camera for *True Grit*. As seen through his lens, the American West circa 1870 has the gorgeous and evocative look of those old and slightly faded hand-tinted photographs.

The Coens' script is actually more faithful to Charles Portis' original novel than the 1969 John Wayne film. The narrator is a middle-aged woman named Mattie. She tells us the story of how, when she was fourteen years old, she decided to avenge her father's murder. Her father had been gunned down in cold blood by one of his employees. And when the man rode out of town on her dead father's horse—much easier than if he had tried to ride away on her father's dead horse—no one from the town pursued him. A quote from a biblical proverb appears onscreen at the beginning; "The wicked flee when no man pursueth, but the righteous are bold as a lion."

Here come the Coens with another moral paradigm. We are presented with an injustice, and we know what happens when an injustice is perpetrated in a Coen brothers movie, don't we? Quote the Dude, "This aggression will not stand, man!"

Mattie seeks out an instrument for her revenge, and finds him in the flea-bitten person of Marshal Rooster Cogburn (Jeff Bridges), a tough-as-nails, not-intimately-acquainted-with-soap, shoot-first-and-don't-answer-any-questions-later type varmint. After much haggling, the chase is on as the killer, a man named Chaney, has joined the outlaw Ned Pepper's gang that is operating in Indian Territory. The marshal sets out in pursuit by himself, but soon Mattie has caught up with him. They are joined by Texas Ranger Mr. LaBoeuf (Matt Damon) who is also pursuing Chaney for another murder committed in Texas. So our unlikely trio head into Indian Territory to find the killer and exact Mattie's revenge. The following two hours are filled with sparkling dialogue, inspired gunplay, ambushes, bushwhacks, gory violence, and many opportunities for Jeff Bridges to steal the film—which he does.

I mentioned Roger Deakins earlier; the film looks great. And the dialogue—much of it lifted verbatim from the novel—is a joy to the ears. I loved the way the characters spoke. People in the 1870s did not speak like we do today—speech was more formal, and the use of contractions was very rare. And folks had better "dicshun." Also, the cultural references that wove their way into everyday speech were a little more highbrow; Dickens and Twain were well known, so that the level of language was quite evolved by our standards. At one point young Mattie is trying to convince the marshal to accept her offer, and he is getting overwrought. She says, "why increase the volume of your voice when you should instead increase the merit of your argument?" Lovely. Wouldn't it be extraordinary to hear that kind of repartee in the House of Commons, where volume of voice seems to be diametrically opposed to merit of argument? These carefully crafted patterns of speech give the movie a formal style that is rarely found in Westerns, and I enjoyed the sound—very colourful if sometimes a little hard to grasp, but the actors handle it very well. This is one of those rare movies that can be enjoyed almost for the dialogue alone.

If you've seen a few Coen brothers films, you know that they sail their ship under the banner of unpredictability. They almost remind me of an outlaw gang of filmmakers: "Hey Marshal, the Coen brothers just rode into town. They're holed up at the Bijou, and they're threatening to screen their latest movie. The townsfolk are mighty skeered."

But here the Coens play it straight; as straight as they ever have. And it works. A good story is always a good story, and the profound moral issues that the best Western films grapple with are just as timely today as they were in the 1870s: might versus right, individual freedom versus social order, order versus chaos, the corrupting power of money, the unrelenting, unstoppable winds of change that never cease to sweep away what seemed immutable, constantly rearranging our cultural landscape. These are the sweeping themes at the heart of the Western, and these are the themes that preoccupy the notorious Coen brothers. Think of Margie, the unlikely heroine of *Fargo*; her character is not that far removed from *True Grit*'s young Mattie. Morally speaking, they are sisters, if not twins.

I was surprised that Bridges' performance was ignored by the Golden Globes. I think this is another highlight in a career filled with highlights. Hailee Steinfeld portrays the fourteen-year-old Mattie. In the John Wayne film, twenty-two-year-old Kim Darby portrayed the fourteen-year-old heroine, although she did look much younger. John Wayne reportedly hated working with Kim Darby who he called "the worst actress I ever had to work with." By all accounts, Wayne was a cranky camper during the making of *True Grit*, his only Oscar-winning performance. At one point he threatened to punch out Robert Duvall if Duvall didn't stop arguing with the director. Hailee Steinfeld does a fine job as Mattie. She is sharp, and in her own understated way, quite a force of nature onscreen. Matt Damon portrays the Texas Ranger LaBoeuf, a role originally played by Glen Campbell in a rather wooden performance. I'm not a huge fan of Damon, although he was very good in *The Informant!* But there is a strange reserve, an emotional flatness to his performance here. Perhaps he made the mistake of studying Glen Campbell's portrayal—he would be more believable as a lineman for the county than as a tough Texas Ranger. At best he seemed miscast and unable to connect with Bridges and Steinfeld. Josh Brolin as the baddie Chaney is solid in a limited role. Barry Pepper, one of my favourite actors, is very good as the outlaw leader, Ned Pepper. But in the end, *True Grit* is the Jeff Bridges show—an atypical Coen brothers film with none of the surrealism or absurdity that we have come to expect. And in typical Coen fashion, it has layers of meaning if one wants to peel away: a strict moralist tale that can be applied to present-day events in the United States, or perhaps a kind of biblical allegory. The Coens have once again spun us a good yarn.

Unknown

(2011)

Unknown is directed by Spanish director Jaume Collet-Serra. He directed his very first feature film back in 2005, the infamous *House of Wax* featuring the infamous Paris Hilton. I included a review of *House of Wax* in my first book because it was a major stinker. I wrote, "you would get more entertainment from watching wax melting than from watching this mess, although it was a pleasure to see the character portrayed by Paris Hilton get a metal rod through the forehead. It made a SSSCHOOK! sound like a spear slicing through cheddar cheese."

Surprisingly, *House of Wax* was not Mr. Collet-Serra's first and last film. He returns in 2011 at the helm of an action-thriller with an international cast: Liam Neeson, American Frank Langella, Swiss actor Bruno Ganz, German actress Diane Kruger (who portrayed the beautiful Helen in *Troy*), and the American actress January Jones. The story is set in Berlin and before it's all kaput at the end of its one hundred and thirteen minutes, several floors of a luxury hotel will be blown to bits and many Volkswagens totalled.

Unknown is a Donald Rumsfeldish kind of thriller; remember him? "There are known knowns. These are things we know that we know. There are known unknowns. That is to say, there are things that we know we don't know. But there are also unknown unknowns. These are things that we don't know we don't know."

At the heart of the plot of *Unknown* lie those darned unknown unknowns. Those things will kill you, you know?

Liam Neeson is Dr. Martin Harris, an American university professor who arrives in Berlin to attend a biotechnology conference. His wife, Elizabeth (January Jones), is with him. Leaving for the hotel, they hop in a taxi and, incredibly, one of his suitcases gets left behind at the taxi stand at the airport. Well, all right. I suppose it could happen, but hang on, it gets better. The script soon transforms itself into a festival of unbelievable plot twists.

The suitcase that has been left behind just happens to be the one that contains his passport and all kinds of vital documents. Now, I'm not much of a world traveller, but do you know anyone who leaves their passports in a suitcase? I have mine on me at all times, even if I'm just going to Burlington, let alone Berlin.

When our hero Martin and his wife get to the hotel and they get out of the taxi, the good doctor realizes that he is missing not just a suitcase, but the critical suitcase. His wife has already gone into the lobby to check in so, incredibly, without saying anything to his wife about the missing suitcase he hops into a cab and heads back to the airport, without telling his wife where he is going.

How do you say "whoa, whoa; hang on there just a minute!" in German? Anyone in his right mind would take thirty seconds to tell his wife that he was running back to the airport. Of course he would. But maybe, being a scientist, his mind doesn't work the way that normal people's brains work.

I don't know. I'm not a scientist, I'm a film reviewer.

On the way back to the airport, the cab he is riding in is involved in a serious accident. No kidding. The cab goes screeching off the road and into the canal. Martin is knocked unconscious but the attractive young woman who is driving the cab (who by the way looks very much like a punkish Helen of Troy) pulls him out of the submerged cab—not only is she beautiful, she is as strong as a Greek goddess. She begins by shattering the driver-side window with one blow of her steering wheel locking device, and then grabs her soaking wet passenger by one arm and pulls him out.

How do you say "Wow, girl. Where do you work out?" in German?

When the police arrive, she disappears into the crowd of curious onlookers. Our hero is in a coma for four days, and when he awakens, he's pretty foggy. But in one of those amazing coincidences that could only happen in this movie, he is sitting up in bed watching the German news when he sees a news report about the big international biotechnology conference that is being held in Berlin. Perhaps there's nothing good on television in Germany, I don't know, but this biotechnology conference is being covered like it's the Academy Awards. As he is watching, he remembers that he is in town to attend that very conference. And then he remembers that his wife is at the hotel and doesn't know where he is or that he's been involved in an accident. Strangely, you see, no one has made any inquiries at the hospital looking for a Dr. Martin Harris who has been missing from his hotel for four days. From this point, the plot not only thickens, it congeals into an unbelievable mess.

Martin leaves the hospital against his doctor's orders and goes to his hotel where he meets up face to face with his wife who does not recognize him, or says she doesn't. Worse, another man is wearing his name tag, claiming to be the real Dr. Martin Harris. Is our hero losing his mind? Is he the victim of an elaborate plot? Is the screenwriter making it up as he goes?

The most annoying thing about *Unknown* is that for the first hour, it is pretty darned good. It hooks us and we want to know what is going on. The performances are solid—Neeson is very believable as the befuddled doctor, and Diane Kruger suitably intense and enigmatic (not to mention sexy) as the taxi driver who gets caught up in the mystery. Bruno Ganz as an ex-East German intelligence agent that Neeson turns to for help is also excellent. Frank Langella pops in about three-quarters of the way through the film as an American colleague that our hero has asked to vouch for his identity and, to put it kindly, Langella is unconvincing—speaking each line as if it were some unintelligible text that he had memorized phonetically. At any rate Langella's performance was the least of my worries by that point because the script had checked out of the Plausible Hotel some time before, and left no forwarding address.

That being said, there are many thrillers—even some great ones—that throw preposterous plot twists (PPT) at the audience while still managing to be engaging. When it comes to PPTs, there is the known preposterous and then there is the unknown preposterous. The whole basis of one of my favourite Hitchcock films, *North by Northwest*, is preposterous: Soviet agents have been keeping close tabs on the mysterious (actually the fictitious) Mr. Kaplan for months, but they have never seen him. If you stop to think about this, it doesn't wash, but it is a necessary PPT if there is to be a case of mistaken identity. Other PPTs abound in this great Hitchcock film; for instance, if you were speaking to someone who suddenly collapsed in your arms, the victim of a swift knife in the back, your first reaction would not be to grab the knife and to hold it aloft, allowing any news photographers who happen to be present to snap your picture—in the crowded foyer of the United Nations no less! But Hitchcock gets away with a lot because *North by Northwest* moves along at a tremendous pace and has such great visual style and wonderful performances that by the time you start thinking about preposterous plot twists, the movie is over and you have left the theatre.

Not so in *Unknown*.

The best thing about *Unknown* is the excellent car chases. We are treated to some top-notch stunt driving. As good as the chases are, however, the old PPTs are on display: when our scientist hero, Martin, and Diane Kruger's character steal a cab to engage a bad guy in a high-speed chase through the streets of Berlin, why is he driving and not her? Martin has never been to Berlin so he doesn't know the city, and the woman sitting right next to him is a Berlin taxi driver, so why-oh-why is he driving? Answer: he is driving because he's Liam Neeson goshdarnit, and do you think that he's going to make a movie where there is a big car chase and he doesn't get to drive? Hello? I don't think so.

The bomb in this movie—because of course something has to get blown up, real good—is one of those cartoon movie bombs that have a big digital display right on the front so that you know exactly how many seconds the hero has before it blows his face off. I'm not sure, but I think I saw Acme printed on the side.

By the time the plot gets sorted out and things are explained and everything that is going to be exploded has exploded, you may have concluded that some things are just better left unknown.

Vicky Cristina Barcelona

(2008)

Woody Allen's directorial career has been on a rollercoaster of public disapproval since the now infamous revelations of his personal life hit the tabloids several years ago. After ridiculing Hollywood in one of his most underrated comedies (the cynically titled *Hollywood Ending*, 2002), he left the United States to make movies in Europe. His last four movies have been filmed on location in European locales: *Match Point*, *Scoop*, and *Cassandra's Dream* were all set in London or France, and now, with *Vicky Cristina Barcelona*, we are off to Spain.

London seemed to be evolving as a comfortable decor for Woody in his most recent films, but in *Vicky Cristina Barcelona* he seems strangely disconnected from Barcelona. Like the two main characters in the film, Vicky and Cristina, Woody the filmmaker gives the audience the impression that he is an American tourist making a movie in a place he finds attractive, but for which he feels little (if any) affinity.

The first thing that struck me about *Vicky Cristina Barcelona* was the underwhelming cinematography. Allen's movies have always featured gorgeous, if not stunning, cinematography. Think of the magnificent images of Manhattan, or more recently *Match Point*, which offered an attractive vision of London. Here cinematographer Javier Aguirresarobe, who has done fine work in the past — his cinematography on the film *The Others* was particularly outstanding — makes sunny Spain and Barcelona look flat and dull. A movie about art and love and passion in Barcelona should be a feast for the eyes. The film looks grainy and underlit.

Scarlett Johansson and Rebecca Hall portray two twenty-something students, best friends, who have an opportunity to spend the summer in Barcelona. Not unlike *Harold and Kumar Go to Whitecastle*, this is Vicky and Cristina go to Barcelona, and because this is a Woody Allen movie after all, both of these attractive young women are searching for love and meaning in their lives. And also perhaps searching for some air conditioning, because Spain in the summer is brutal.

Vicky (Rebecca Hall) is a no-nonsense type. She is engaged to Doug, a broker in New York. At least I think he's a broker; he has one of those vaguely described jobs that Allen's characters often have, occupations that mostly seem to involve talking a lot on a cell phone. Most of Woody's characters seem to have jobs that pay them lots of money and allow them a ton of leisure and vacation time. Woody has never been the filmmaker of the working class. Anyway, Vicky is working on her Master's thesis: The Catalan Identity. This immediately struck me as suspect. I mean, The Catalan Identity isn't a thesis, is it? It's a pretty broad subject. A thesis would be more like Existential motifs in Catalan Painting, wouldn't it?

Cristina is portrayed by Scarlett Johansson. She is the opposite of Vicky: wild, unpredictable, and emotionally adventurous. We are told that she has spent the last year making a twelve-minute movie that she hates, and that she has come to Barcelona with Vicky to recharge her batteries and have an adventure. When one character asks her what her twelve-minute movie is about, she describes it as a story of multiple and often contradictory patterns of love, or some such drivel; I am paraphrasing. As a film critic this amused me, because I know very well that exploring multiple and contradictory patterns of love in a movie takes at least thirty minutes.

The amorous adventure Cristina has been waiting for comes along in the form of Juan Antonio (Javier Bardem), a painter who propositions the two women one night in a bar. No-nonsense Vicky is shocked and insulted; Cristina is fascinated. She agrees to fly off with Juan for a weekend in Orvieto. A very reluctant Vicky tags along for the ride.

Woody cheerfully stirs the pot, and the plot soon attains the dramatic thickness of a rich Marinara sauce as no less than three love triangles are explored. Vicky and Cristina both fall in turn for Juan Antonio who is still in love with his ex-wife, the fiery Maria Elena—portrayed with formidable style by Penelope Cruz. We learn that Maria Elena once tried to kill Juan by stabbing him, but yet, he is still in love with her. Well, I suppose if your insane and murderous ex-wife looked like Penelope Cruz, it is possible that you could still be hooked.

After his disturbing turn as the psychotic killer in *No Country for Old Men*, Javier Bardem has a relative walk in the park with this role, and he seems to be thoroughly enjoying himself while sporting much better hair. Scarlett Johansson, Rebecca Hall (Sarah in *The Prestige*), and Penelope Cruz add considerably to the visual appeal of the film.

Gossip break: Bardem and Cruz became an item on the set of *VCB* and were married in 2010. As of this writing, they are still together and have a young son named Leo. Cruz won an Oscar for her performance in *VCB*, making her the second Spanish actor to win an Oscar. The first was Bardem who won for *No Country for Old Men* in 2007.

Patricia Clarkson, a fine actor in her late fifties, portrays a woman who has been left standing at the proverbial dock of life, watching wistfully as the last *Love Boat* sails off into the sunset. Her character's only raison d'être is to repeat to Vicky that she is also going to miss the soul train if she doesn't follow her heart and do something adventurous. "You will be miserable and racked with regrets for the rest of your life," she tells her solemnly.

Vicky Cristina Barcelona is neither straight drama nor true comedy. It has an artificial feel to it. I could best describe it as a fable; a film bursting with every romantic movie cliché and bustling with well-to-do, idle people—architects, investors, an abstract painter—all with no money concerns in the world. The film is also coloured (or marred) by tacky narration. I have no idea why Woody thought that this movie needed narration. The narrator (who is never identified) keeps telling us things that we either already know or that we have seen onscreen, so what is the point? Is Woody the filmmaker talking down to the audience because he fears that his narrative is a bit muddled? Also, why have a narrator who is neither a character in the story nor omniscient? Whoever he is, he often just sounds like someone reading from a mediocre romance novel. If the intention of having a narrator is to make the story seem somehow more believable, the device fails completely. This story would not be believable if the narrator was Alexander Solzhenitsyn.

At seventy-three, perhaps Woody Allen has had an epiphany of sorts. After directing forty movies in forty years, he may have come to the conclusion that the illusion of reality that he has often strived so hard to achieve is completely superfluous. With *Vicky Cristina Barcelona*, he seems to have concluded that it matters not in the least if the events unfolding onscreen are believable or not, or if the characters stay in character, or if the events portrayed are wildly implausible—the audience is going to gobble it up anyway, and cheer and sniffle and laugh because life is just one big soap opera. It seemed to me totally absurd that Juan would not only let his fiery, nutty ex-wife, a woman who tried to kill him, back into his life but then also encourage her to enter into a love triangle with him and Cristina. But perhaps that is Woody's take on the stereotypical fiery Latin temperament—you just never know what those hot Latinos are going to do. At best this is caricature; at worst it is cartoonish. But I do have to admit that no one can throw a temper tantrum like Penelope Cruz. As Bart Simpson would say: "Ay Caramba!"

There was some advance buzz about this movie because of a rumoured sex scene between Scarlett Johansson and Penelope Cruz. Some of you may be disappointed. It is hardly a sex scene. Scarlett Johansson and Penelope Cruz do have an erotic encounter in a photographic dark room, but nothing actually develops.

Sorry.

The scene feels tacked on. Perhaps borrowing a page from David Lynch's playbook—Lynch is well known for including gratuitous sex scenes in his films (see *Mulholland Drive*)—I had a hard time convincing myself that this scene constituted a vital plot element, propelling the narrative boldly forward. The term "voyeurism" springs immediately to mind. I am afraid that I have to conclude that this steamy encounter occurs because it might be good for the box office. Of course, given the choice between watching gratuitous violence or gratuitous sex, well . . .

The film is good fun, at least for its first hour. The bad news is that even at a relatively economical ninety-six minutes, the movie still feels too long. That being said, there is always something of value in a Woody Allen movie. Penelope Cruz steals every scene. In her tight red dress she reminded me of a large firecracker—and she acts the part. And I thought I detected a thinly veiled auto-biographical reference: when the narrator tells us that Cristina felt that America was too mired in conformity and consumerism to correspond to her "freer vision" of what life could be about, I couldn't help but think that this might be Woody explaining himself.

Vicky Cristina Barcelona is entertaining—a good rental, certainly, but the DVD would be much improved if it allowed the viewer to mute the narration.

W.

(2008)

As George W. Bush entered the last months of his presidency in 2008, a film was fanning the flames of an already overheated presidential election campaign. Oliver Stone's *W.* purported to reveal the truth about George W. Bush.

It is with more than a little trepidation that I approach any new Oliver Stone film, and just the thought of reviewing it can be enough to make me queasy. You just never know what you're going to get with "the Stoner." He reminds me of Rich Garcés who used to pitch for the Boston Red Sox a few years ago. His nickname was "El Guapo" (Spanish for The Handsome One). On the mound, El Guapo vacillated between brilliance and complete ineptitude—practically unhittable one inning, and a veritable "base-on-balls" machine the next. Indeed, from one batter to the next he could go from pinpoint control to couldn't find the plate if he was sitting at the dinner table. I think of Oliver Stone as the El Guapo of directors. And when he's really bad, I think of him as "El Guano" (Spanish for dung).

But he's made some great films! I can hear you say.

I don't know if his first film, *Platoon*, was really great; I haven't seen it in over twenty years so it's pretty foggy. But he has certainly made some bizarre, and profoundly flawed films. In 2004 he gave the world a stinker of epic proportions, *Alexander*, which contributed to our understanding of Greek history almost as much as *Bedtime for Bonzo* contributed to our understanding of Darwinism.

Unlike *Bedtime* (which of course starred future President Ronald Reagan), *W.* features some terrific actors. Ellen Burstyn as Barbara Bush and Scott Glenn (Al Shepard in *The Right Stuff*) as Donald Rumsfeld are both excellent, melding seamlessly with their characters. But not all of the performances are as successful. Thandie Newton portrays Condoleezza Rice as a cartoonish figure. Her characterization transforms the Secretary of State into a faithful, manic little mouse whose vocation seems to be to scurry around her beloved boss while emitting little squeaks of approval. I always found Condoleezza to be kind of creepy, particularly when she got on her high warhorse to pontificate icily about Saddam, but in Newton's hands she seems about as creepy as Minnie Mouse, although with much more stylish clothes. The script never overtly explores the tabloid rumours that circulated concerning a possible affair between Bush and his Secretary of State, but the puppy dog look that Dubya gives "Condy" in one scene practically shouts, "race you to the Oval Office; woof, woof!"

Oliver Stone seems to have a real flair, if not genius, for coaxing terrible performances from otherwise talented actors; Kevin Costner's hyper and unintentionally funny turn in *JFK* is a case in point. In fairness, however, Costner was wrestling with a script that was practically booby-trapped. The seemingly endless scene that has him repeating seventeen times, "This was a coup d'état!" would have reduced even the greatest thespian to a mound of quivering Jell-O. And for sheer weirdness, nothing could ever top Kyle MacLachlan's wig in *The Doors*, but Newton's performance in *W.* is certainly one of the most demented to be found in any Stone film.

While *W.* may not be Oliver Stone's big comeback, it is at least entertaining. And I'm happy to say that Josh Brolin tackles the title character with great panache. Anytime you make a film about a major public figure, and especially one that has been caricatured to the extent that Dubya has, you play with fire. Helen Mirren pulled off a real coup when she portrayed Queen Elizabeth in *The Queen* (2006). And you might recall that Michael Sheen who portrayed British Prime Minister Tony Blair in that one was similarly excellent. James Cromwell was superb also as Prince Philip, and he shows up in *W.* as George Bush *père*. He gives a solid, no-nonsense performance. But the success of the film ultimately boils down to whether or not Josh Brolin can create a convincing portrait and avoid tumbling into caricature. It is easy to portray Bush as a cartoon character, but Stone is really trying to get at the true nature of this stumbling, bumbling, mumbling president. Could he possibly have been as dim as he sounded? Did everyone just "misunderestimate" him all those years? Who is the real Dubya? Is this perhaps Oliver Stone's answer to Conrad's *Heart of Darkness*? Is this *Heart of Dumbness*?

I hate to say this, but the script beats around the Bush quite a bit.

Actually, I enjoyed that.

I mean that the narrative is rather messy. The story bounces around between the post-9/11 era and Dubya's formative years as a partying child of privilege in college—a hard-drinking, neer-do-well failing (and giving up) at all kinds of endeavours. He meets his future wife Laura in college, portrayed by the cuter-than-cute Elizabeth Banks. The young Dubya is shown as someone who loves to drink (all the time) and who loves to talk (all the time) with his mouth full. Stone's camera treats us to lots of close-ups of half-chewed food. In other words, Stone thinks Dubya is a slob. It quickly becomes a complete mystery to the audience why a bright and attractive woman like Laura would be interested in "Slobbya," but she is, and the rest is history.

The script, by Stone and Stanley Weiser, proposes a classic case study of a chronic underachiever never being able to live up to his successful father's lofty standards. For Stone, this is the key to understanding not only the inner workings of George W. Bush, but also to understanding why the United States in the wake of 9/11 plunged so recklessly and enthusiastically into a war with a country unconnected to the attacks. Stone would have us believe that George Jr. was thrilled to death at the idea that he might upstage Daddy and finish the job left unfinished in Iraq (i.e., take out Saddam and install a new regime). There are times when Stone almost seems to feel sorry for Dubya as he portrays Donald Rumsfeld and Vice President Dick Cheney as the real powers behind the President—crusty, hard-as-nails men who manipulate poor Dubya into thinking that he is truly making the decisions. "I'm the decider," he tells Cheney at one point, when in fact he is little better than a puppet.

I have a bit of a problem seeing Dubya as a kind of stooge to Rumsfeld, Cheney, and Paul Wolfowitz. I can't believe that Dubya didn't know what was going on—a scene where he is shown to be profoundly shocked that the intelligence about Iraq's Weapons of Mass Destruction was completely wrong seems totally unbelievable. Perhaps that's the problem with making a film about extremely sensitive issues while the principal players are still on the stage—Stone had to temper his comments and pull his punches. I think Stone hopes his movie will help the Democrats, but he doesn't want to sound too strident. If he wanted to make a difference, he should have made this movie before the 2004 election.

Colin Powell is portrayed as the lonely voice of reason, the only temperate soul amid the boisterous war mongers of the Bush inner circle. Yet, in the end, despite his grave doubts about the reliability of the intelligence reports, he agrees to play along. In the light of his misgivings, the speech he gives to the UN to justify the American war plan is less than enthusiastic. As portrayed by Richard Dreyfuss, Dick Cheney exudes a kind of sinister efficiency. Taking the spotlight during a strategy meeting, he launches into a five-minute monologue that is chilling in its implacable vision of how America can and should establish an Empire—nothing less—in the Middle East; taking absolute control of all desirable territories and resources. After this scene, there is no doubt that Cheney is the mastermind.

Given the richness and dramatic potential of the events portrayed, I regret that the script seems more informed by the tabloid press than by the *Washington Post*—brimming with tired psychobabble about a man desperate to win his father's love. Dubya's conversion as a born-again Christian (helping him to overcome his alcoholism) is portrayed in a fairly convincing manner. What I found pretty scary is that Stone obviously believes that Dubya *believes* that God had chosen him for a higher calling. The problem with our leaders holding such beliefs is obvious: if someone truly believes that they are doing God's work, they can never be wrong or be diverted by sober second thoughts. Once you believe that God is on your side, anything — invasion, war, mass murder, just about anything at all — can be justified.

But perhaps the biggest sin that Stone commits in *W.* is one of omission. The paramount question of how it came to pass that such a personage became president in the first place is all but ignored. In a dream sequence near the end of the film, Bush Senior alludes to "that situation in Florida that we fixed for you," but that is the extent of Stone's interest in the subject. I would have thought that Stone's polemical nose would have been positively twitching with excitement at the prospect of exploring the massive election fraud that seems to have led Dubya to the White House. For a director who has devoted a great amount of screen time to conspiracy theories much shakier than this one, he really dropped the football here.

—   —   —

Several years after the release of *W.*, Josh Brolin was still fuming about the criticism the film received from many Republicans who never even bothered to see it. Denying that *W.* was a hatchet job on the former President, Brolin declared, "We wanted to know the guy that never should have been president and probably should have run a baseball team — and been very happy doing it."

Many people would have been very happy if George W. Bush had been content to run a baseball team. And many people, both Americans and Iraqis, would still be alive.

Why We Fight

(2005)

Transparency.

Canadian voters heard that word a lot during the 2006 federal election. Under Stephen Harper's leadership, a Conservative government was going to be much more transparent.

I think that the Conservatives lived up to their promise. I feel like I can see right through them.

I don't want to be any more cynical than I have to be, but it does seem like Western governments are somewhat less than transparent these days. And it is exactly this question of transparency that is at the heart of Eugene Jarecki's compelling documentary film *Why We Fight*.

Why We Fight is thematically related to Michael Moore's *Fahrenheit 9/11*, but I think that Jarecki's film is much stronger because it exudes a transparency, if not an objectivity, that Moore's incendiary films never even attempt to achieve. The weakness of *Fahrenheit 9/11* was that it was so strident and sensational that it alienated—scared away, actually—the very people who should have paid more attention to it. Sadly, it was dismissed as propaganda by many who never even saw it, and it failed to make the impact that it should have. I have no problem with propaganda, especially if I happen to agree with it, and it's not like the *other side* doesn't bombard us with propaganda, but if the goal is to change people's thinking or at least to encourage them to reconsider a particular situation, the filmmaker has to give the film some veneer of objectivity. *Why We Fight* does this.

"Is this an important film?" is the question that often pops up when the conversation turns to politically charged documentaries.

What does it mean if I say a film is important? For starters, it means that I think the film is useful and enlightening. *Why We Fight* makes a very compelling, well-reasoned argument about why America went to war in Iraq. The film also explores the much larger question of why the United States seems to be perpetually involved in one armed conflict after another. More pointedly, it illustrates how the official reasons given for justifying involvement seem to be dubious at best.

Jarecki makes some very powerful points, beginning with a discussion of President Eisenhower's farewell speech in 1961. Eisenhower was a military man, but he was also the first person to warn us about the military-industrial complex; it was the first time that now well-worn phrase was used in a public speech. Extraordinary.

Think about it: a president leaving office, a man who spent almost his entire adult life in the military, a four-star general, warning the American public about the dangers of having big business and big industry unite with the military and start to dictate American foreign policy. Up to that time, it was believed that foreign policy should be predicated on America's own defence or the defence of its allies or whatever was in America's best interests. But what would happen if foreign policy came to be determined by the profitability of certain conflicts? What if armed conflict was the real economic engine of the United States?

Excellent use is made of archival footage to explore the history of America's armed conflicts since WWII. Many talking heads provide input: ordinary Americans, ex-military people, and journalists. One of the most powerful moments of the film occurs when a retired New York City policeman is interviewed about the war in Iraq. This man's son was killed in the September 11 attacks and he, like millions of other Americans, has supported the war in Iraq because, in his words, he believes it to be "payback" for September 11. He believes — or has been led to believe — that Iraq was involved in the attacks and was a source of terrorism. The shock on this man's face when he hears President Bush declare that there was no link between Saddam Hussein's regime and September 11th is shattering and emotionally naked. Stunned, he looks straight at the camera and says, "What is he, nuts? If Iraq wasn't behind 9/11, than what the hell are we doing there?"

One of the most thoughtful statements in the film comes from US Foreign Policy critic Chalmers Johnson who says, "The defence budget is three quarters of a trillion dollars. Profits went up last year well over twenty-five percent. I guarantee you: when war becomes that profitable, we're going to see more of it."

I would encourage everyone to approach *Why We Fight* with an open mind. The filmmaker believes that the American government, and this could be said of most Western governments, is waging a campaign of disinformation against the press and the public. I am not enamoured of conspiracy theories, but I do believe that systematic government control of information has reached unprecedented heights. *Why We Fight* is important because it asks the tough, vital questions. The film borrows its title from the famous series of propaganda films that were directed by Frank Capra during WWII. Back in the forties, it wasn't hard to make a case for "why we fight" when the enemy was Adolph Hitler and he had invaded most of Europe. These days, however, when confronted with murky, complex, and volatile situations like those in Iraq and Afghanistan—and with the constant fear of terrorism in the air—there are no simple answers to "why we fight."

Jarecki's film also explores the thorny question of who gets to fight in these dubious wars—a question that Michael Moore also explored in *Fahrenheit 9/11*. You may recall the scene in *Fahrenheit 9/11* that showed two Marine recruiters aggressively canvassing an economically depressed neighbourhood. In *Why We Fight*, a military analyst tells us that "there is a growing gap between the composition of the American military and the middle and upper classes. There are quite simply many more recruits coming from impoverished or socially depressed backgrounds."

Why should this be so? If we take for granted the idea that the children of wealthy people have less chance of being killed in a war, then surely there is something profoundly wrong with the system. I think that my ancestors the Gaulois had the right idea:

when there was a conflict between tribes, the chiefs fought it out. No civilian casualties. War as we know it would simply cease to exist if our leaders had to actually fight each other. When it's your own blood being spilled, you get a whole new perspective.

Even though *Why We Fight* won several awards at various film festivals, it barely registered on the radar when it was first released. And when it did receive some distribution, it did not do well at the box office. I believe that people would have been very interested if they had known about it. I am obviously naive.

American moviegoers—not to mention American film distributors—seem to have very little interest in films that aim to stimulate informed discussion about foreign policy. War is a monstrous waste of money, resources, and human life, and yet movies that tell people that their government has lied to them, and continues to lie to them about the real reasons that their kids are being placed in harm's way just do not seem to be able to get widespread distribution or to generate audiences in any significant numbers. Case in point: *Why We Fight* and *Scary Movie 4* arrived in theatres at about the same time. *Why We Fight* opened on six screens and grossed $53,000 its first weekend. *Scary Movie 4* opened on 3,602 screens and grossed $40 million its first weekend. Now that's really scary.

Winds of Heaven

Emily Carr, Carvers, and the

Spirits of the Forest

(2010)

Despair is part of every creative individual. It can't be con-
quered. One rises out of it. I suppose we are only content
when all our sails are up and full of the winds of heaven. I
hope all your sails are up and full of the winds of heaven.
There is only one way. Keep on.
—Lawren Harris, from a letter to Emily Carr

Emily Carr is a Canadian art icon. And that is part of the trouble,
or at least it was before Montréal-born writer-director Michael
Ostroff made this beautiful and revealing film. The problem is always the same: when you're an icon, people think they know all
about you. For too many people, the name Emily Carr conjures
up the image of an elderly, stout, and dour curmudgeon—Emily the eccentric, Emily the crazy lady living in her trailer, Emily
the circus sideshow with her little monkey. The complexities and
contradictions of life and spirit are reduced to their most simplistic form. The icon becomes caricature; the caricature becomes the
accepted truth.

According to the director, the goal of the film—we could even
speak of a mission—was to reveal the heart and soul of Emily
Carr. But while Carr's rollercoaster life occupies centre stage, the
film paints a broad and engaging picture of the white community's

treatment of Indigenous peoples as well as its extreme ambivalence toward Indigenous culture. I use the term "ambivalence" rather than "hostility" because, as *Winds of Heaven* underlines, the Canadian government (through its agent the National Gallery) latched onto Indigenous culture as a cornerstone on which to build its concept of a truly Canadian identity, while at the same time dedicating itself to the assimilation and eradication of the very culture it was, supposedly, celebrating. Only in a severely schizoid country would we mobilize our bureaucracy to obliterate all outward traces of Indigenous culture while at the same time carefully relocating totem poles and Indigenous artifacts to be proudly displayed in museums as "proof" of our Canadian identity. Watching the opening and closing ceremonies of the 2010 Winter Olympics in Vancouver, I was struck by the irony of it all—we portray ourselves to the world as culturally unique by usurping the trappings of Indigenous culture, but when the crowds leave and the cameras turn away, we continue to treat our Indigenous peoples like second-class citizens. *Winds of Heaven* quietly but forcefully makes the point that while the National Gallery realized that Indigenous culture was a major component of an emerging (or fabricated) national identity, the government's own bureaucrats were enforcing policies, like residential schools, aimed at assimilating Indigenous culture out of existence.

Emily Carr described herself as "a friend of the Indian." She understood Indigenous culture as well as any white person with a similar background could have, but she was a product of Victorian society, and even though she rejected much of its value system, she also had misconceptions about Indigenous culture. One of the film's many strengths is to reveal the complexity and contradictions inherent in Carr's relationship with the West Coast Indigenous culture that inspired her most powerful visual symbols. As the film unflinchingly points out, Carr understood Indigenous culture, but she also misunderstood it; yet more than any other Canadian artist of the time, she sensed on a spiritual and visceral level the great power that lay dormant in the totem carvings that she depicted. The wild, dark, and primal spirit of the forest was also her touchstone—a force that both exhilarated and frightened her—and John Walker's superb cinematography draws us into her paintings to convey the sense of deep spiritual connection that she felt when communing with nature. A film whose visual power is much amplified by a large screen, *Winds of Heaven* allows us to vicariously walk around inside some of Carr's most powerful works, and by extension, to walk around a bit in Carr's own shoes.

When it comes to using archival film footage to flesh out a story, Ostroff is a master. The portrait he paints of the times is both engaging and dynamic. As mentioned before, Carr's own paintings and sketches are lovingly explored, as is the beautiful West Coast of British Columbia—John Walker won the Robert Brooks Award for Documentary Cinematography for his work on *Winds of Heaven*. Rather than have an actor portray Carr—a rather clunky device that has marred many documentary films—the director chose to have Diane D'Aquila read (off-camera) Carr's own words from her personal journals and letters. This technique really brings Carr to life. D'Aquila gives a superb reading, and Carr's presence is strangely amplified by her absence—we are only occasionally shown a pair of hands drawing or painting. Carr seems more present in this way, her voice speaking to us like a confidante, disembodied yet vivacious, as if she were hovering just outside of the frame, very much alive.

In *Winds of Heaven* we get a real sense of Carr's personality and artistic vision. The artistry of the film is that it manages to pull off a most difficult conjuring trick; it makes visible to us that most invisible of qualities—the spirit that moves the artist.

The X-Files:
I Want to Believe

(2008)

Fans of the defunct television series were overjoyed that series creator Chris Carter decided to strike again with another big-screen adaptation. The first *X-Files* movie, *Fight the Future*, was released in 1998 and it did very well, both commercially and critically. Directed by Rob Bowman, it featured all of the key elements that made the series so popular: aliens, a government conspiracy (you might recall that the plot dealt with the aliens trying to insidiously colonize the earth) and some terrific guest stars including Armin Mueller-Stahl as an evil ex-Nazi.

An evil ex-Nazi — is there any other kind?

Also along for the ride were series stalwarts well-manicured man and the smoking man, and Martin Landau appeared as jack-in-the-box man — the name I give to the character that always pops up out of nowhere in all of these conspiracy movies to explain to the audience what the heck is going on. In Oliver Stone's *JFK*, that role was played by Donald Sutherland.

ATTENTION: Major spoilers ahead. This time around there are no aliens. Darn. No government conspiracies either, but this *X-Files* movie — with its mad Russian scientists performing monstrous medical experiments — is vaguely reminiscent of several other horror films like 1985's *Re-Animator* and even the classic *Bride of Frankenstein*. David Duchovny and Gillian Anderson reprise their roles as Mulder and Scully and this time they are involved in an intimate relationship, except that you have to wonder about any couple that call each other by their last names. On the other hand, Mulder's given name is "Fox" so we perhaps understand why Scully might prefer to call him Mulder. Anyway, Mulder and Scully are in fine form here, and if the movie works as well as it does, it is because Duchovny and Anderson have great onscreen chemistry and give strong, believable performances.

As our story begins, Mulder and Scully are retired from the FBI. We learn that Mulder is being harassed and threatened with prosecution by the FBI on some trumped-up charges. He now sports a beard and works hard at maintaining his privacy. In other words, he has become a bearded semi-recluse. Scully is working as a surgeon in a Catholic-run hospital. She is a brilliant surgeon (naturally!) but she is struggling with the case of a young boy afflicted with a rare, and seemingly incurable, brain disease. The hospital where Scully is practising is called Our Lady of Sorrows. Leave it to Catholics to come up with a really depressing name for a hospital, as if it wasn't depressing enough to be hospitalized. What's next, Our Lady of Infinite Cold Sores? Whatever happened to cheery names like Our Lady of Hope, or Our Lady of Mercy, or Our Lady of Really Yummy Hospital Food? That's where I want to go if I get sick.

Our Lady of Sorrows is run by a musty Catholic order, and the crusty head priest who chairs the Board of Administration seems to have been hired exclusively to engage in moral and theological debates with the brilliant but agnostic Scully. Never mind that it is farfetched in the extreme that Scully would be working in a Catholic-run hospital—this is only happening because the script needs to set up a major conflict over an experimental stem-cell treatment that may be the only hope for Scully's young patient. In fact, stem-cell research is at the heart of a plot that quickly thickens when we witness the brutal kidnapping of a thirty-something woman. She is taken by two men as she gets out of her car on a snowy night in West Virginia. It turns out that this woman is an FBI agent, and the FBI doesn't take kindly to their agents being abducted. So the FBI tries to rehire and reunite agents Mulder and Scully as they bring Mulder in to consult on the case. The script piles it on, bringing in a convicted pedophile, a former priest named Father Joe (Billy Connolly), who claims to have visions that might help the authorities find the missing agent. The FBI turns to Mulder's expertise to determine whether the priest is a real psychic or just a real nutball. Connolly does a fine job playing this apparently tortured and repentant psychic priest, and his inimitable Scottish brogue adds colour and texture to the ever-thickening plot. When another young woman is kidnapped, the plot—having by now attained the consistency of Scottish oatmeal—becomes almost opaque. Mulder becomes convinced that the priest is a legitimate psychic, while Scully remains skeptical and openly hostile to this convicted pedophile. The FBI is increasingly skeptical toward everyone. Meanwhile, back at the Sorrows, things are getting mucho bumpy as Scully must decide whether to go ahead with a highly risky and painful stem-cell treatment for her young patient.

I haven't even mentioned the evil Russians who are perverting stem-cell technology for their horrific experiments. These mad Russians are actually behind the kidnappings. Taking a page from schlock movies like *The Brain That Wouldn't Die* and *They Saved Hitler's Brain*, the Russians are only using the bodies of the kidnapped women—attaching the head of their leader to the freshest body available to keep him alive. Yuck. The only thing missing here is a hunchbacked assistant. Exactly why they only use the bodies of attractive females to keep the head of their male leader alive remains unclear, but it may well have something to do with sustaining the interest of the males in the audience.

The X-Files: I Want to Believe feels like a superior television episode—an Emmy-calibre episode. The story held my interest, and the performances are excellent. I was disappointed of course that the plot was devoid of aliens—almost any movie is elevated by the presence of aliens—but I think that Chris Carter has crafted an engaging thriller. The plot does have some holes in it, though: when Scully's car, a white Ford Taurus, gets totalled in one scene, it shows up in the driveway in perfect condition later. How is this possible? Was the car sent to Area 51 for repairs? Is that the secret the government has been guarding—they are holding living aliens in Area 51 and using them for top-secret automotive repairs?

Put *that* in your conspiracy pipe and smoke it.

About the Film Critic

Robert Fontaine grew up in the sixties in a house where movies were woven into the family fabric—all-night marathons at the drive-in and Saturday matinee double bills were treasured family outings, eagerly anticipated and energetically discussed afterwards. In retrospect it seems inevitable that he would gravitate toward film studies and broadcasting. Robert has been a freelance writer-broadcaster for the past twenty years, reviewing films for CBC Radio and covering jazz for Radio-Canada in Ottawa. Passionate about movies and music, Robert is also a working drummer and has led his own jazz quartet since 2009. Married, he lives in Gatineau with his wife, Sylvie, and their son, David. Their large Lab mix, Buffie, enjoys light classical music and watching Wallace and Gromit cartoons.

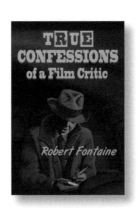

TO ORDER MORE COPIES:

GENERAL STORE PUBLISHING HOUSE INC.
499 O'Brien Road, Renfrew, Ontario, Canada K7V 3Z3
Tel 1.800.465.6072 • Fax 1.613.432.7184
www.gsph.com